Only in Brussels!

Mihaela Gherghişan

ONLY IN BRUSSELS!
A politically incorrect journey through Brussels' times

Editura Excel XXI Books
2017

Editura Excel XXI Books
Calea Floreasca 167 Etaj 4
Sectorul 1
013725 - București
www.exxibooks.ro
office@exxibooks.ro
comenzi@exxibooks.ro

Coperta: Vasile Baltac

Descrierea CIP a Bibliotecii Naționale a României
GHERGHIȘAN, MIHAELA
    Only in Brussels! : a politically incorrect journey through Brussels' times / Mihaela Gherghișan. - București : Excel XXI Books, 2017
    Conține bibliografie. - Index

32

A day in Brussels

One Saturday morning in Brussels, on a quiet street in the residential area not far from the Schuman roundabout, a bag was snatched from an old lady shoulder and taken for a ride on a bike. The lady started screaming after the snatcher who could not hear her anymore as he was heading towards the roundabout.

Little did he know that that Saturday a second day of an EU summit was about to start. Police fences had been put in place since the previous morning and they were guarded by armed men.

As the petty thief speeded through the empty streets right into the fences, the police, thinking that this was an attack against the EU leaders, opened fire against him.

The guy fell off his bike still holding tight to the old lady's bag. He was hurt and an ambulance was called. The police took some time to understand the misapprehension. A panic started to grow among the armed forces protecting the Schuman area.

Not long afterwards, the Reuters agency sent out a wire: *"An attack against EU summit is underway"*. The agency later corrected the piece and added the entire information on the facts.

When I got to the press centre in Justus Lipsus later that day, an Estonian colleague and friend read to me the whole story and then look up from his laptop and told me in a grave voice: *"Only in Belgium!"*

He didn't know it then, but I think he will agree with me now, that this story was both funny and sad for more reasons than one.

The little impact that we think the EU has on our lives

The EU makes such a small impression on us, citizens that we almost forget it is there. It is as if we ever knew about it.

2

The petty thief that ran away on his bike right into the EU Summit closed area didn't know of any gathering that day in Brussels. And why should have he known?

The EU Commissioners are protected by bodyguards and go around in secured cars, but no one ever tried to kill any of them.

Over the past 50 years, two incidents related to an EU Commission official are accounted for, but you'll see why they don't count.

The first was a failed attempt, in the sixties, to murder an EU commissioner who was mistaken for someone else.

The second was an accident that an EU Commissioner had while driving himself his armoured car. The car proved to be too difficult to manage; he missed a turn and finished his ride in the window of a store.

And forget about the remote places in Europe that never heard of Brussels other than being the nest of terrorist. Instead, just ask anybody in Brussels what the EU is all about and don't smile if he or she is surprised by your question.

"EU? Europe you mean?' one woman told me when I recently did the exercise. *"Oh, that? I think is there where all the good jobs are!"*

A young man thought I was making fun of him; he smiled to me and said: "*C'mon lady, what are you trying to prove?*"

An old lady said she was pleased with the EU. "*My sister rents a house to a sweet couple that works for Europe. They always pay their rent on time!*"

Another young man had heard of Erasmus. Now, that's a good thing, he said, a friend of him spent two years abroad, was it Italy? "*Yeah, good thing, but now that the English want to leave, it's going to be different*". He couldn't say why…

So why don't we know about "*Europe*"?

Each time the EU institutions decide to spend some money on communication, they put out brochures, emails, videos or gifs which are all starting with the same sentence: "*did you know that the EU does (pays, is responsible for, has brought to you…, etc.)?*"

Questions are immediately spreading to my mind each time you come across these messages: "*How are people supposed to know that?*" Or, more to the point: "*why are they supposed to be interested in that?*"

The EU, meaning the EU institutions or the member states, is financing infrastructures, economic and social programmes, etc. which are supposed (and sometimes even manage) to improve our lives.

But Brussels does a lousy job in communicating the real effort put in place every day for the citizens. All it does is to employ an army of communicators who, once they got the job, lose all contact with reality and start producing incomprehensible materials.

EU also demands that each project funded with EU money to be advertised as such. Whenever you travel down a road which has been financed with (your) EU money, a big sign placed on the side of the road is informing you about that. These gigantic billboards, crafted like the ones indicating the road works, always failed to impress people.

The EU, like all projects, should reach the people through media. The information role of the press has always been fully recognised by the EU institutions.

Media campaigns, press conferences, press releases, working conditions for the media, they all exist. More than eight hundred journalists and technicians are accredited to the EU institutions, sometimes more than a thousand gather for EU summits.

But how many times have you found in recent years an article about the EU on the front page of a newspaper? How many times does a news program open with information about an EU Summit? When you log on to your Facebook account, do you often see an EU related matter being discussed?

EU is present in the media and in the social media (especially on Twitter) and you can see it if you follow the right accounts. But if you're not working in the Brussels bubble and you're not a journalist interested in the EU affairs, there are very little chances that you'd do so.

Brussels was somewhat known for being the home of the EU Institutions and the centre of the EU (sometimes soft) power. Now, Brussels is known for being a nest of terrorists.

This piece of bad news has travelled fast across Europe and replaced the other one in people's minds. In space of several hours following the 2015 Paris attacks, Molenbeek, the Brussels municipality home to a terrorist cell, was known across the globe.

Brussels, as being the art deco capital of a small kingdom and the heart of Europe and also home to the NATO headquarters, almost ceased to exist.

French media could not pronounce properly Molenbeek. British media placed it outside Brussels. In the East, where values of tolerance have not yet reached the minds, people were cursing Islam and told us to get out of this *"odd place"*.

Then the American President called Brussels *"a rat hole"*. This could unfortunately be a powerful image.

The *"EU in Brussels"* lost all exposure when another attack was perpetrated in 2016, this time right in Brussels. The news travelled again extremely fast and it was also instantly broadcasted in the American media.

One of the bombs exploded in the subway, few metres under the EU Commission's main building. Some of the media underlined this, some didn't. So EU was not even important when it appeared to have been targeted in a terrorist attack.

In 2014 the Belgian police uncovered a plot of two terrorists travelling from Syria through Turkey who intended to blow up the EU Commission. They were arrested as soon as they landed in Brussels.

The news only became available several months afterwards and it produced a big laugh.

Blow up the Berlaymont? Given the little knowledge people have about the institutions and their location in Brussels, they could've ended up blowing up the Committee of Regions by mistake! The plot was uncovered during the month of August, which means that even if they would've gone ahead with their plans, they could've only shaken an almost empty building.

What can I say? EU does not sell whatever the effort put into selling.

The problem of too much communication

The EU has, since always, produced news worth events, but these are all technical and difficult to understand. This is why we need specialised journalists to translate it into something that people could understand and even be interested in.

We therefore need the press to get the people to realise why it is so important.

But the press often gets confused or cannot reach the right information. There is a lot of *"noise"* around the institutions, there is a lot of *"communication"* going on, but the quality of it is not what it should be.

Let's have a look into it.

The main institutions of the EU have different ways of communicating.

The European Parliament has a *"directorate general"* meant only for communicating. In addition to that, each political group and each committee has its own communicators.

Every Member of the EU Parliament (MEP) has its own team of assistants whose job is also to keep in touch with the national and the European press. Tens of press releases are sent out daily during the monthly plenary session of the Parliament in Strasbourg.

In 2014, prior to the last European elections, the Parliament spent €6 million in advertising through the media. €121 million were spent across EU Member States for outdoor advertising focused mainly on transport hubs like airports and railway stations as well as the public transport.

That did not stop the decline of the pro democratic parties in their performance in the elections. In 2014, the most unlikely set of new MEPs entered the EU Parliament, shifting the centre of attention towards the right and the left extremes.

The EU Commission has another way of communicating, this being the only institution having a daily press briefing.

This daily pointless exercise called *"Midday"* gathers in the Commission's press room several journalists (not too many nowadays) and most of the spokespersons, but gives away very little useful information.

Agendas, announcements for the day are happily communicated, but when it comes to comments or position on different political or even technical files, the lips are sealed.

Here also an army of communicators is at work, they also depend of a *"directorate general"*, but since Jean-Claude Juncker was *"elected"* president of the institution, things have changed.

The spokespersons' number as such has declined, since each spokesperson is now in charge of several big files. They are assisted by nameless and faceless people called *"press officers"*. They can gather information and send it to the media, but they can never be quoted.

And a parallel set of communicators has entered the stage since 2014. These are the members of EU commissioner's *"cabinet"* dealing with their boss' image and presence in the media. They can be bothered for details on a specific subject or even asked to facilitate an interview, but they cannot be quoted either.

The Council of the EU, the other big EU institution, relies much on the member states-led communication.

And as little we tend to think of the EU's image makers nowadays, as big is the impression that national Permanent Representations to the EU make on us. They are top diplomats managing the EU affairs for their own country.

Most of the spokespersons of those representations come back as ambassadors in several years. They are well trained, fully equipped for the harsh job and very well connected in the Brussels bubble.

The way we were...

Allow me to be sentimental about it.

Back in the years 2000, I remember a totally different atmosphere around the press rooms in Brussels. Those older than me can tell you about the Jacques Delors years when the Berlaymont building (the star-shaped construction on round about Schuman) was both home to EU Commissioners and journalists.

Legend has it that one can also park underneath the building if he was a press card holder. The intimacy between the eurocrats and the press was complete.

Myself, I remember the moment when the EU Commission was relocated in a smaller building, down the road from Schuman, on Avenue d'Etterbeek. It is called *"the Breydel Building"*. There were fewer commissioners then, all of them packed up at the 12th floor.

There were fifteen EU member states and the bigger ones like Germany, France and UK had two EU Commissioners. In all, the institution was represented by 21 politicians, including its President.

The EU Parliament had only 500 MEPs and it occupied the same buildings as today, in Brussels and Strasbourg.

The European Council had only the Justus Lipsus building and it did fine. The Europa building (right next door) was, at the time, known as the building A of the big 1920s complex called Residence Palace.

The complex, a former high standing apartment building, built between the two wars and occupied by the Nazis in 1940, was partially reshaped in 2001. The building C has become home to the accredited press in Brussels. It still has the original swimming pool and a theatre, both located in the basement, both out of use.

The building A went into transformations soon afterwards and many, many years later has become the ugly piece of modern architecture known as Europa building. It hosts the EU summits since 2017.

In Breydel, the press room, located in the basement, was much smaller than the one we now have in Berlaymont.

The Berlaymont was, at the time, under total reconstruction due to traces of asbestos found in the walls.

The lobby of the press room in Breydel was a tiny place with few chairs and tables and it still allowed smoking.

From the lobby, a hidden pair of stairs took you to the first floor were the spokespeople's offices were located. The access was free for journalists who were seen there every day just knocking on open doors and chatting freely with the spokespeople.

Say you wanted to speak on the record with the EU Commissioner. That wasn't easy, but it was manageable. Otherwise, if you wanted a statement on the record right away, a spokesperson received you in his office or he sat down with in the lobby.

Many an afternoon I spent there with colleagues and spokes just chatting or working. The lobby of the press room was the place to be during those years. People were nice, friendly and helpful.

The cosy atmosphere created there by the small size of the place and the good mood of those people was irremediably lost when the EU Commission moved back into Berlaymont in 2004.

But while it lasted, some ten years or more, it was bliss. Even so, I remember that the chat about how little people understand from our reports was going on.

The middays were extremely useful and one could go there like going to school in order to learn, to exchange information and to connect with others. I don't think we ever connected to the outside people, though…

The spokespeople were professional and mostly in good mood. And don't forget these were difficult times too.

The Santer Commission collapsed in 1999 in the first ever corruption scandal of this size and was replaced by the best team Brussels ever saw before or since: the EU Commission team led by Romano Prodi.

In 2001 the Belgian EU Presidency wanted to reinvent Europe. This was one of those full hearted presidency prior to the Lisbon Treaty, the one which invented the job of EU President and took away the power of national presidencies.

The Belgians had gathered in South of Brussels, in the Maison d'Erasme, people like Umberto Eco, Borislaw Geremek and Agnès Jaoui for a brainstorming. Never again there was so much bliss around the EU project.

The invitation was addressed by the young and spirited Belgian Prime Minister Guy Verhofstadt who hadn't stoop yet to the level of a EU Parliament group leader, completely disconnected from the reality.

I repeat: they were not happy times altogether. The war in Bosnia had finished after it had generated the worst atrocities Europe had known since War World II. Another atrocity was about to take place in Kosovo in 1999 and Europe was about to miss another chance to be a peace bringer.

NATO, led by the American ambition, conducted air strikes against Serbia for three full months. This led to a number of problems, especially human tragedies and the bigger role sought by the EU in the Balkans.

The corruption scandal that brought Romano Prodi to Brussels has continued to generate mistrust between the EU institutions. One of Prodi commissioners, the German Michaela Schreyer was brought in front of the Budgetary Control Committee of the EU Parliament (the COCOBU) in 2003 as Edith Cresson was some years before. Schreyer very nearly lost her position.

Whistle blowers were spreading in Brussels. Paul van Buitenen and Marta Andreasen were delighting the press with stories about how much the EU Commission spends in the wrong places.

But the most unnerving of all was the year 2001 that had the very near victory of the extreme right in the French presidential elections in May and of course the terrorist attacks of 11 of September.

That day, Europe thought it was on the verge of something new. Something unexpected had happened and it weakened the mighty USA. EU thought of that as an opportunity not only to stand by its American friend and partner, but also to demonstrate its moral superiority.

The American hegemony, heavily criticised in some parts of the EU (like France), had just back fired and some politicians here, on the old continent, were glad.

France had just opposed the strikes against Serbia and it continued to oppose other American plans, like the invasion of Iraq in 2003. Like France, other EU nations thought that following the American way was bad and that the only way forward was the deeper integration of the European dream and the EU enlargement.

Therefore, the enlargement to twelve new member states, foreseen for 2004 and 2007, was seen in Brussels by some as a kind gesture towards the Central and Eastern Europe, one to be thankful for.

15

When in 2003, the French President Jacques Chirac learned of the support of countries like Romania, Bulgaria and Poland for the invasion of Iraq, he was furious. *"They missed a good opportunity to shut up"*, he told us during a press conference in Brussels.

And least, but not last, Europe was confident in the way it dealt with its minorities. Back then, the problems with the ethnic minorities in the EU were to be found in Romania and Hungary. They were *"accession countries"*, so they couldn't know about the civilised way in which to deal with the matter.

They were given examples of good practice to follow like the integration of the Swedes in Finland. France, as it doesn't recognise the concept of *"minorities"*, could not lecture them on this topic too.

And France did not know it then and Belgium, Germany and UK didn't know it either, that poor integration of their own minorities was going to back fire too. The home grown terrorism we deal with now has its roots not only in the conflict in Syria, but in the doubtful way in which big western democracies have dealt with their Muslims communities.

But we were all unaware of the difficult times ahead and we were all of us, politicians and media, gently living and working in Brussels, creating a better future.

How little we knew and how unprepared we were!

During those years the big EU enlargement was the main subject in Brussels; the communication on it was almost perfect, but we criticised it. Things were going well, there still was a European project on the table and people were really struggling for Europe, but we thought they didn't do it right.

In 2002, the Copenhagen EU summit wrapped up the enlargement. Last minute negotiations were held the entire night between the Danish Presidency and the Polish Prime Minister, Leszek Miller.

A media circus was created around Miller as his demands for money were getting bigger by the minute. He wanted the Polish farmers' rights to be settled there and then. He did not leave the table until he got €1 million right away (instead waiting an extra year for it) as well as bigger direct payments for the farmers.

His demands triggered others from other future member states and the summit became a market place of vanities. It was a sad display. The press cashed in on that. Criticism abounded. We thought that the EU and the politicians reached a new low.

Looking back to that moment now, we can only smile.

The Danish released a documentary in 2003 about those six months spent at the top of the EU. The film has little commentary and original sound bites in

Danish, English, Polish and even bits of Turkish and Russian are heard.

The camera spared no one, politicians and media alike and all the glorious or the embarrassing moments are shown. The Turkish visit to Copenhagen amid reticence for the Turks throughout the EU, the embarrassing summit between EU and Russia in Brussels, the bargaining of the EU enlargement: it's all in there.

A veteran French journalist watched this documentary again recently and confessed that it brought tears to his eyes. He realised that in spite of all shortcomings or failed negotiations, these were the last happy moments that we had as united Europeans.

The trouble was that we did not know it then. We were unhappily getting by events and information. Politicians, media, public, business men and women, nobody understood Europe as it was.

But we had some hints…

We were interested in foreign policy. We were following closely the Middle East and the Maghreb countries. The UN summits on famine and poverty really found a striking cord in the middle of the EU too.

The American dream (being a good thing or a good thing) was an interesting topic too.

But when things started to degrade here, at home, when the economic crisis hit and then Brexit and terrorism shook us badly, we became interested exclusively in ourselves.

And even this interest is an uneven one.

Think of the agriculture topic: this use to be not a big, but a huge issue since the creation of the EEC. The Common Agriculture Policy reform in 2002 has drowned all the deserved attention.

The agriculture marathon meetings in Brussels that had to answer French farmers demands without delays have prompted the press to stay up all night. Agriculture ministers' gatherings in Brussels (and sometimes in Luxembourg) were still a page turner. Hundreds of pages were written, reports on television were available, radio programs were dedicated to the farmers. Not any more…

None of these were reproduced afterwards, not during the next big reform in 2014 and not even during the milk crisis which saw thousands of milk producers repeatedly threatening to burn down the EU Commission building (and once almost burned down the EU Parliament by mistake).

Abandoned by the media and the decision makers in the same time, the farmers nowadays have no one to turn to, although they are experiencing the hardest times since the World War II.

So how come we lost interest in the ones who feed us? How come we only talk about Brexit and Donald Trump these days and we forget all the other topics?

Journalists or followers?

The experienced Brussels based journalists –the veterans- are well connected beyond the press services. A friend in an office, an ambassador, a secretary can be a gold mine of information. The journalist would know how to use it and how much to those use as to inform and never harm.

The veterans also know how to avoid being manipulated by the *"too nice"* sources which apparently give away information for no hidden reasons.

The veterans or the representatives of the Anglo-Saxon media are also indulged with leaks. The institutions-controlled leaks are a way of communicating. This is not the best way, of course, but it can suit both the eurocrats and some of the journalists.

And how much of it reaches the public?

The big press articles and materials produced in Brussels announcing mergers that are to be approved or rejected by the EU Commission, the last minute agreements or betrayals happening between the groups in the EU Parliament are fun.

They promote a journalist in the first ranks of the media body and attract both respect and jealousy. The agreements reached after hours of negotiating between closed doors are also fun to write about, especially if they are the lasts in a long series of *"breaking news"* already announced before the meeting.

But let's face it. None of these are page turners. None of this really means anything to the citizens.

People read and are impressed by human being stories and events that they can get a grip on. The cruel summer of 2015 when Greece was nearly kicked out of the euro was one of the rare moments when people really connected to what was going on in Brussels.

For many, this was a catastrophe on the making, they were witnessing the collapse of a project called the euro, the same euro that they had in their pockets. This was real, tangible, a piece of news regarding the endangered stability of ordinary European households, whether they plainly understood the situation or not.

This is the odd nature of the news: the bad ones sell while the good ones often go unnoticed. When people paid attention to the ministers of finance gatherings in Brussels during those days (as well as to the huge rally against Brussels going on in the same time in Athens), the piece of news was bad. Bad for Greeks, bad for the EU and bad for the people of this Union.

It was not easy to put in plain words what was really going on and why Greece got so close to the edge, but the headlines were: *"Ultimatum for Greece"*, *"Greece facing expulsion from the Eurozone"*, *"Eurozone collapses in Brussels"*.

Did you know about the circular economy and more to the point, about the EU Parliament's resolution on this? Did you notice that the member states approved important issues concerning the Agenda for Security?

This news came out in the time as the Greece deadline that summer. They were important, but not threatening; also, they were technical, difficult to understand and difficult to sell. They went unnoticed because most of the journalists snubbed them.

The Brexit vote the next year and the statements that followed in Brussels were also widely followed. And no matter how many reassuring statements we are going to hear in Brussels and how much journalists report about the *"orderly retrieval of the UK from the EU"*, the markets are still going crazy over Brexit.

Other news from Brussels, the ones we sometimes write, just don't sell. So we stop selling them

So what do we journalists do?

When a freshly arrived journalist is trying to make his way into the Brussels bubble, he or she will try to present facts and information interesting for his home country. He or she will almost without fail start reporting on technical matters, but on human being stories too.

The French will go for the French investor in Belgium who set up a business in Wallonia, the Romanian will try and find a trucker whose wages don't fit the market, the Polish will go for compatriots making it to the top in the EU bubble, the Brit will find British people applying for the Belgian citizenship.

This is all nice and good, but after a while of attending *"Middays"* and rubbing shoulders with spokesmen, diplomats and others, he or she will start speaking like them. After another while, he will start thinking like them. Before the year is up, the fresh correspondent will find himself reporting on technical issues and reporting on the same issues as anybody else.

We have all started by wanting to be interesting. We all ended up being boring.

The problem is that when we are based for too long in the same place and we only travel to EU events organised elsewhere but on the same pattern, we never distance ourselves from the facts.

Just recently I was asked whether I was a pro Europe journalist. The question seemed tough, but fair so I decided to answer it. But when I opened my mouth, instead of words, out came just a nervous laughter: I realised that I don't really know the truth about that. All I could finally say is that I'm too close to the subject to even realise if I still entirely like it or not.

So we're boring and we know it. Some of us really tried to be different. And failed…

When Politico first came to Brussels back in 2014, they promised to be the best media that the bubble has ever seen. They started with a fresh approach by questioning the system. The task was fun and pleasant and it was also easy.

Weakened by the poor performance of the pro Europeans in the EU elections and after a change at the top of the EU Commission, the institutions were an easy target.

The extreme right was already pointing its nose for the upcoming elections in France and Brexit was on its way. The member states were also weakened.

Politico made a great job in putting the system into question. It questioned the efficiency of Juncker's team and pointed to the poor performers of some of his commissioner (we all remember the articles about Corina Crețu). It went into the EU Parliaments corridors, heard rumours, questioned the faith of veteran MEPs. It went into the deep thoughts of national diplomats gossiping about Juncker.

The fun lasted for a while. Then Politico entered the lion's cage and attacked *"le bras droit de Jean-Claude Juncker"*, his Cerberus and chief of *"cabinet"*, Martin Selmayr.

Martin does not have many friends in town, so the articles about his reign of terror in the 13th floor of the Berlaymont were an instant page turner in the bubble.

Politico, first despised due to its aggressive attitude when it first anchored in Schuman, gained the respect of some political circles and media representatives. Not long afterwards, being the victim of it success, Politico went further and started speaking to Juncker's team, on and off the record.

But the *"off the record"* part did not go well. The journalist reporting on the latest Selmayr's deed in November 2016 could not prove that Commissioner Kristalina Georgieva told him that she was leaving the team because of Selmayr. She denied ever meeting anyone from Politico and called the publication *"a gossip rag"*.

This casted some doubt on Politico's credits, but it didn't prevent it, in the end, to be the most read publication, according to a Burson Masteller's study released in May 2017.

In autumn 2016, in a transparent attempt to *"make peace"*, Selmayr accepted a live chat on Facebook under Politico's auspices.

The deed was done. That day Politico entered the Brussels's bubble for real. It has transformed into another boring Brussels reporting media, always present when a bone is thrown from the table.

We, journalists, tend to think that we are making a difference here in Brussels. But let's be honest, how many of us ever achieved that?

There is no investigative reporting from Brussels. All we do is listen to what we are told and report on it. It doesn't really matter that we find nice words to translate the rough information into or that we are making fun of the news. In the end of the day, we realise that we all have waited for the bone to be thrown.

Two moments in the bubble history are standing out from this point of view: Commission Santer resignation on 15 of March 1999 and the exposure for corruption of four MEPs in May 2010.

Both were media-led events and happened thanks to investigative journalism.

The first was due to a series of articles written by André Riche and Jean Quatremer and published in the Belgian Le Soir and the French Liberation. The affair was one of corruption and it concerned the

French EU Commissioner and former Prime Minister Edith Cresson.

At some point, the Committee of Budgetary Control (COCOBU) of the EU Parliament questioned the affair. Cresson could not account for part of the money spent on false contracts and she was asked to step down. When she refused (as instructed by the then French President Jacques Chirac), she dragged the entire team with her into the drain.

The events have promoted both journalists to fame; nevertheless, André Riche later preferred an EU Parliament job to the one he had with the Belgian media.

But these were the older days when the Parliament did not have as much power at it has today, but acted as if it did. Now that it has power, it chooses not to use it.

When Politico exposed Corina Crețu in 2015 and the COCOBU was supposed to question her early in 2016, the meeting was eventually cancelled.

COCOBU said it was pleased with the written answers it got from the EU Commission secretary general on the matter, which were somewhat ambiguous, truth be told. And that was that.

The second was the work of an investigative team from Sunday Mail that travelled to Brussels in order to frame the corrupted MEPs. They obtained appointments with them disguised as lobbyist and proposed money for amendments to laws being discussed at the time.

The conversations, during which four out of ten MEPs accepted the transaction, were taped by a hidden camera.

All framed MEPs stood trial. The journalists were severely criticised in the bubble because of the disguised they used, but the story was soon forgotten. Some of us came to their rescue and filed stories about how their act was righteous since this was the only way to expose the corrupted practices going on in the EU Parliament.

The policy of leaks

Brussels has always survived on leaks to the media. Without them, life here would be really dull.

But why do we have them and to whom benefits the crime?

When I first started to report from Brussels, some twenty odd years ago, the leaks were not frequent, but big.

For some time, I thought that a good, nosy and intelligent journalist can obtain these through hard work. Then I started to realise that wit and professionalism had very little to do with it. It was whom you represent that mattered.

In the beginning of this century, the leaks almost exclusively concerned the EU enlargement.

A colleague and friend working then for the British media (now a spokesperson for an international organisation) was treating us with delicious stories obtained directly from the EU Commission files.

There were juicy details about what the Commission intended to do with Romania (my main interest at the time), about the laicism in Turkey and the latest push for the Poles.

My friend and colleague was manipulating papers having the EU Commission's logo on the header and a stamp across the text which read *"Restraint EU"*.

I thought she was the luckiest, most intelligent and most professional person in the world. I also thought that she was the kindest when one evening she photocopied some of those papers and gave them to me.

I admit, it took some time for me to understand that when the EU Commission does something *"courageous"* or at least a bit controversial, it also needs to test the market in advance.

There are clear situations in which a subject better be dropped. In 2008, the college of commissioners led by José Manuel Barroso abandoned a homosexual rights related issue as it was clear that the public opinion in Germany and in the East was not favourable. It did not even draft the proposal.

But for many other cases, it went ahead with the draft occasionally mentioning it to some *"trusted"* journalists in the bubble. In later stages, parts of the draft are published (maybe not as such) in some *"trusted media"*, like Financial Times or Reuters. Sometimes Financial Times Deutschland is the beneficiary or even Der Spiegel.

The reactions from the capitals are then expected to give the green light or to put the brakes on the process. The capitals usually targeted are Paris, Berlin, London and sometimes Rome. Others count much less.

The leaks, although infuriating, are the best way in which the Commission navigates in stormy waters.

The institution, although it changed dramatically over the past twenty years and had three different presidents, has always claimed to fight against the leaks. The hypocrisy of the situation seems to grow by the year. The bigger the trouble with leaks, the bigger the statements against them.

Sometimes it gets tricky.

Martin Selmayr, when he took up his position with Jean-Claude Juncker in 2014, was already well aware of that practice. He also knew that some journalists will do almost anything to be included among the *"trusted"* ones.

It was during the period right after summer when Juncker was interviewing his future commissioners and the bunch gathered in Brussels was as high in colours as it was controversial. Speculations on who will be the Czech, the Spanish, the Romanian and the British future EU commissioners were going hysterical.

Martin thought of a joke and put it into practice. He gave to Euractiv a false piece of information, a false list of portfolios and told them that this was for their eyes only.

Euractiv published it, of course, and created a turmoil in countries like Romania where they thought that Corina Crețu got the *"humanitarian aid"* instead of the more glamorous *"regional policy"*. Some say that the wicked idea of misleading the journalist (and eventually the public) actually belonged to Juncker himself.

Beware of eurocrats when they are bearing gifts.

The EU Commission is the champion of leaks because it holds the monopole of the initiative in the EU. The EU Parliament or the Council are the ones targeted by the leaks, since they could pour cold water on Commission's projects.

Therefore, it is easy for the EU Council President Donald Tusk to criticise the practice. *"I don't want to be part of this new political culture of permanent leaks,"* he told reporters at some point when he thought he had enough.

He was actually referring to uncontrolled leaks that can also occur.

The German press was again treating us with comments made behind closed doors. This time it was about an unfruitful conversation between the EU and Donald Trump in Brussels. The week before, it had been the case with *"a disastrous"* dinner that Juncker had with Theresa May.

"Today's diplomacy needs professional plumbers rather than indiscreet diplomats," he added, probably referring to the Polish plumbers that were about to be scrapped from the Western market by a severe *"services' directive"* drawn up by Juncker as Emmanuel Macron expected him to.

And Jean-Claude Juncker is also infuriated by his commissioners because they talk too much and they also go out on Twitter.

He has been criticised by the press because he practically never comes down to the EU Commission press room to hold a proper press conference.

"I don't need a press conference", he is reported to have said. *"I have college meetings"*, he added referring to big mouth commissioners who tell their national press everything after those meetings.

There are ways in which a journalist from the bubble could get a hold of confidential information without being manipulated.

The personal relations developed by him or her are therefore crucial. The social life in the bubble is also extremely important. The juicy piece of information is never too far for those who know whom to listen to and how to listen.

The EU is there to stay, but doesn't shine

I once met a woman at a party in Brussels who had just come back after a ten years long leave from the EU Commission.

The institution had to take her back and found her a cosy place in the Employment Directorate. She told me that she was extremely happy about her job and that she was looking to buy a really expensive house in Brussels.

Then she politely asked me about my work and found out, with astonishment, that I report about the EU. *"And do people want to know about that?"* she asked gasping for air. I said that I know how to get them interested in the matter and she smiled disbelievingly. *"I don't see how! I mean, I work for the EU and I'm not interested in what the EU does!"*, she pointed.

I must say, in that moment I felt like I was having a field trip. So, the legends are true! The EU's civil servants are really lazy and bad and they are too well paid for not doing anything!

I smiled back and said: *"I thought you loved your job…"* *"Oh, yes, she agreed, we had such a wonderful party last Friday in the office!"*

Here is one story that I like repeating each time I like to infuriate someone. The EU civil servants blush and say: *"We are not all like that"* while the non-civil servants jump to the ceiling: *"See, I told you! They are the worst!"*.

The truth, as always, is somewhere in between and this story only illustrates how little we know the EU as such. It also shows how badly damaged the EU's image is, even among those who work for it.

In the eighties, Peter Ustinov said that the people often criticise the UN because they get annoyed with what they see about the Security Council meeting or the General Assembly in New York *"which is really like quarrelling about something which goes on in a shop window"*.

"What goes on inside the shop is usually what people don't see (…) they do an extraordinarily amount of very good work", he explained.

This could be applied to the EU; bad news sells and we, the journalist, like to emphasize all the failures of the EU meetings (especially of the EU summits), the result being that people get annoyed with the EU.

So not only people know little about the EU, but the things they know are very rarely positive.

It is true that many of those meetings ended up in a quarrel or without a shadow of result during these past ten years. It is a shameful display for the EU to see all that effort put into nothing and to show such lack of unity at times. But it is the work behind the scene that often matters.

Like the UN agencies, the EU's staff really tries to make the right things and at the right time. Things usually don't get nasty at that level, but at the political level. EU, like the UN, being an organisation based on democracy, could not in fact function any other way.

It is also true that if EU does a lot of great things for the people, it has also failed to deliver when people expected it to do so.

It is unclear what EU does when it does best and it is painfully clear when it fails.

Whose Europe is it, anyway?

The lack of clarity about EU's advantages was not a problem as long as people were warming in the Brussels's *"sun"* without ever questioning its efficiency. When things were more or less good, when people had jobs and could travel, what was the point in asking where do the benefits come from?

Most of us probably just assumed that they came from our states. Then, as the EU's role got bigger and bigger, we sometimes heard of it without really understanding what the fuss was all about.

It is, of course, a little different in the eastern Europe where the aspiration of being part of the EU was huge after the communism collapsed; there, people really thought that that the EU was the promised land. This and NATO.

But even in the East, the enthusiasm fell to decent levels once the big enlargement took place.

Then the financial crisis occurred. It was shortly followed by the economic crisis. And then the terrorist attacks brought another sort of crisis.

None was overpowered by the EU which simply lacks the means and sometimes the will to tackle the new, modern, big and unprecedented threats.

Crisis after crisis

The bank crisis came as any crisis would: unannounced and unforeseen by any analyst. This was the piece of news about the EU that people found out about immediately and sometimes understood.

Being bad news and also very personal, it didn't need much explaining: we were all in danger of losing our savings as well as our jobs.

We woke up one morning and found ourselves in the biggest mess we have ever seen in our lives. Our grandparents lived through the crisis of the 1929, but this was history and not the kind of history which repeats itself. Or so we thought…

And what was Europe doing to protect the people? How do we sail through the storm?

"We must save the banks!", the answer finally came from Berlin (after some consideration of the matter) and then from Brussels. As much as the idea was probably a good one, because it saved people's money along with the banks, it was also a difficult one to apply.

To this day, those times remain controversial times. And, as this was not enough, the EU as whole – as much as the Eurozone – was forced to save the Greek economy too.

Here it got really tricky for EU leaders, like Angela Merkel and Jean-Claude Juncker (also President of the Eurogroup at the time) as much as for José Manuel Barroso and others.

How do we explain that after cheating for such a long time with figures, Greece not only gets no punishment, but gets to be bailed out? *"The Greek tragedy"*, as the press not so cleverly named it, lasted for several years, the country returned on the bond market only in July 2017.

So is the EU a good thing or a bad thing? Whom is Europe actually protecting? And if it is doing that bad, should the EU get bigger, brighter and more political?

It's somehow funny if we think about it: the fear of starvation brought the Europeans together in the fifties and the same fear drifted them apart fifty years later.

It is not however hard to explain this: when countries were not tied together, they thought that unity will give them strength. But too much unity brings fear of loss of sovereignty and of loss of identity. Too much of a good thing can be a bad thing or it can be perceived as such.

Eurostat, the statistical office of the Union is periodically releasing results of surveys that show a steady percent around 60% being in favour of the EU.

This figures should put our minds at ease about EU's health. But do people really understand the questions?

The Greek crisis and the bank crisis led, among others, to the creation of the banking union that cuts the existing ties between the banks and the states. Therefore, placed under the same huge umbrella and supervised by independent banking authority, the banks could no longer endanger the sovereign debt.

But people's knowledge of the crisis starts and finishes with it. Unlike the bank's crisis, the banking union, being too complicated to explain and also too technical, almost never made it to the front page.

It is funny in a sad way that people understood more about the EU from un unwanted events, like the Greek crisis and Brexit, than from all the information campaigns ever imagined by Brussels.

When the United Kingdom decided to abandon the ship, there we are, all over sudden we are all of us Europeans and committed to the European values and we stand united against London.

But several years prior to that, when the EU was granted the Nobel Peace Prize, nobody understood why. *"And don't give me that crap about the EU creating a continent of peace! We are at war, aren't we, with the banks!"* a young journalist told me.

And, as those problems were not big enough, the migration crisis started in 2015 and it is not about to end soon. The little solidarity left in the hearts of the Europeans was already dried out during the Greek crisis, so when the migrants reached in massive number the Italian and the Greek coasts, nobody wanted them.

So what is the EU all about?

It used to be about one single big market, terribly boring, but terribly useful. Only few people know how it works, but it's there and this is probably a good thing. When Brexit will come along in 2019, this wonderful bureaucratic creation will be shaken like never before.

It used to be about free travel set up by the Schengen agreements that only some member states (like UK and Ireland) didn't think it was appropriate. The migration crisis put an end to the Schengen area as we knew it as more and more states have closed their borders.

It used to be about the single currency, the euro, a practical invention that added comfort to our lives, as much as it inflated the prices when it was first introduced. The Greek crisis and the financial crisis have shown how fragile the euro can be.

So what is left there for the citizens of Europe?

Erasmus, the student exchange programme that could not live up to its obligations when the crisis began? The common single foreign policy that could not stop the annexation of Crimea by the Russian

Federation and turned the former soviet republics away from Brussels?

There is one tangible aspect of the EU that people might tell you about if you stop them in the street and ask them: the bad image given by José Manuel Barroso and Jean-Claude Juncker together with the huge salaries paid to *"faceless"*, *"useless"* employees of the EU in Brussels.

Barroso left Brussels in 2014 after ten years spent at the top of the EU Commission, but in 2016 we found him being an advisor to the Goldman Sachs for Brexit.

The ethic committee of the EU was asked to look into the matter and found that there was no reason to sanction the former EU Commission president. The man had waited for the legal period of 18 months before he embarked into his new position.

How simple is that? So a man who clung to power during ten years in an extremely well paid job with the EU, then chose to work for the bank that did its bid in order to shake the Greek economy and endanger the Eurozone. And of all the topics available, he chose to advice on Brexit.

The EU Commission employees were furious. They set up a group which demanded sanctions against their former president. No sanctions were taken to this date.

Barroso's shoes in Brussels were filled by Jean-Claude Juncker, a true European, sincerer and more dedicated to the EU project than his predecessor. Juncker was supposed to have had the job instead of Barroso in 2004, but he denied it then.

In 2014 he seemed to be the right choice again. But why was he looking for the job?

Juncker did not leave the national politics in 2013 because he lost an election, but because he resigned from the Prime Minister job following claims that he failed to stop security agency activity such as phone-taps and corruption. He had been at the top of the Luxemburg government for 18 years.

During this time, claims are that he also transformed the country into a tax-haven whose potential is bigger than any other tax haven in the world as, unlike others, it benefits from the European free movement of capital.

Nick Cohen wrote for The Guardian in 2014 an analysis about this man:

"I admit that Jean-Claude does not appear at first glance to be the man most likely to promote the European socialists' goal of "ensuring that our societies become fuirer". Nor at a second, third or fourth glance either. Juncker has dedicated his career to ensuring that society becomes less fair"

Concerning the EU civil servants pay, this is no longer a cliché that upsets the EU civil servants (not all of them working in Brussels), but it is what people really believe.

The salaries are high, much higher than in the national public services and there is a reason why is so. But people don't want to know about reasons and are uninterested in these kind of calculus and explanations. All they know is that somewhere in this Europe someone does maybe less in order to be paid more.

People are under the misapprehension that in the EU institutions nothing ever happens. Can we blame them? Has anyone ever tried to explain what really goes on in those offices? And does anyone know how to get a boring bureaucratic reality into something that people may want to hear about?

As improbable as it may seem, most of the EU's civil servants work hard most of the time. They not only do paper work and pointless meetings; they actually draft projects that can be beneficial for the entire EU.

The trouble with their work is that more often than we think it is put aside once it reaches the member states. Lots of good projects from Brussels are rejected by the states and therefore, the overall achievements seem meagre.

In addition to that, the Brussels bubble is not attractive to the untrained eye. Blocs of concrete and steel and glass piled one in top of another, ugly urban architecture, what is there to like?

Perhaps if a couple of cats like Larry from 10 Downing Street and his archenemy Palmerston from Whitehall were to be found in the bubble, people could get interested in the place.

Imagine that this could only be possible, that each institution would have its mascot and that the mascot would have its Twitter account.

NATO headquarters in Brussels are proud of Oscar the Cat which greeted the press during the NATO Summit in 2017. The feline has no spokespurrson and no Twitter account, but it's there and that's a start.

But are we safe?

Since the terrorist attack against the Jewish Museum in Brussels in 2014 and up to now, we almost lost count of all attacks against the Western part of Europe.

The extremely sad thing is that our politicians knew about the threat as the secret services have warned them. The foreign fighters that left France, Belgium, Germany and UK to go to Syria were coming back. They were disabused, trained, puzzled and full of hatred. They were looking for revenge.

So the EU politicians started talking about them and meetings have piled up all through 2013. In Brussels, several interior ministers met in the summer of 2014, they were representing the countries from where the foreign fighters left for Syria. Their discussions, hosted by the Belgian Interior minister, have remained classified.

In more or less the same time Belgium learned of a Belgium national having reached Syria. He was filmed while killing *"enemies"* in Syria. Images also showed him laughing and threatening the world in the same time; he was behind the wheel of car who was supposed to drag corpses of people he had just killed.

The images, shown on Belgian television, were shocking. The man, the authorities knew little about, was born and raised in Belgium, he was of Morocco origin.

His name was Abdelhamid Abaaoud. He returned to Belgium, set up a terrorist cell in Verviers, near Liège, and coordinated the Paris attacks in November 2015. He got killed two days afterwards in Saint Denis. His little brother is or at least was in Syria. Belgium has lost track of him completely.

But prior to November 2015 attacks, in September, a workshop of EU justice ministers was held in Brussels. Their discussions were extremely interesting. They came together to exchange good practices of dealing with terrorism and radicalisation.

Several things emerged from their talks: Belgium was fully aware of the danger and was about to set up different practices, the Nordic states were aware of very little, but they were willing to learn, France thought it had everything under control and did not seem to see the real threat. The French justice minister was the one who left the meeting early, she only stayed for an hour.

Two months later, France was about to be proved wrong. Attacks in Belgium, France again, Germany, Sweden, UK, Spain and Finland followed.

Each time it happens, the EU puts out the same press statements. We have compared them. They are all the same, almost to the coma, what changes is the date and the town or the people they are referring to. And the words lost their meaning: *"shock"*, *"horror"*, *"condemnation"*, *"grief"*, *"unity against terror"* don't mean a thing anymore.

You may or may not know, but EU has a coordinator for the fight against terrorism. The position was introduced in 2004 after a bomb exploded in Madrid and was first held by a Dutch politician, Gijs de Vries.

Mr. De Vries only stayed on the job for three years and step down in 2007 because he did not wish to renew his contract. In short, since nobody listened to him and his position was not a powerful one, he simply left.

The Belgian professor Gilles de Kerchove took up these duties then and he is still on the job now. De Kerchove is a brilliant mind, an elegant old fashion academic who once told me that he never used public transportation in his life.

The man has repeatedly warned against the danger of terrorism in its various possible forms, but was never heard. He was invited to attend various EU ministers meeting, but his reports were never fully taken into account.

To the Belgian media, to whom he exclusively spoke up to 2015, he confessed he never met the MI6 top people and that the security services of the member states did not interact with him.

This all changed somehow after November 2015, but his wit is still not fully used. His position and his reports don't bring much changes into the EU policies against terror, should they exist. He is merely a spokesman for the EU's resolve against terrorism.

His interviews have multiplied, almost every journalist in Brussels has had the opportunity to meet this former discreet man.

To all, he explains how much the EU does against terror: coordination of national policies (previously non-existent, although we thought they existed), improvement of the legal framework including the definition of terrorism accepted on a EU level (it is incredible, but we didn't have one), cooperation with Eurojust (with who???) and deradicalisation programs (each country has tried his own ideas, none worked).

This is all nice and good, but when I asked him in November 2016 if he would feel safe in the subway in Brussels, he laughed very hard. He then admitted that he was surprised by the question. He finally gave an answer: *"Yes, absolutely, and I'd go to crowded places too. The risk of an imminent attack in Europe is very low"*.

How many attacks were there since then? Four? Five? And how many people died? We almost don't count them anymore...

So what are the national states and the EU doing to protect us? How united is Europe against terror?

We don't see any of the great ideas stated in the statements also put into practice. We don't see unity, resolve, shock and terror when it comes to politicians' actions. We only see young, scared armed men patrolling on the streets of Brussels and Paris: they are there for our safety and to remind us that we are actually not safe at all.

In the aftermath of the Paris attacks we learned that national services did not communicate and did not exchange information on criminals and potential dangerous individuals like they were supposed to since the creation of the Schengen area.

50

The area was thought to be one of free movement and security, but only the bid about the free movement was true.

The only Paris attacker who survived came back by car to Brussels that very night without being arrested by the French police, although they stopped the car he was in. The reason? They didn't know him: the Belgian police did not communicate soon enough information about him to the French police.

We also learned that the somehow utopic idea of creating a European CIA was really a utopia: such thing will never exist.

So what is the EU actually doing to stop the terrorist phenomenon?

There are indeed some improvements in cooperation between capitals since 2015, there is a legal framework for combatting terrorism and attempts to cut the financing of terrorism, but with very little result.

Since the attack in Oslo in 2010, the EU has tried to combat solitary wolves that get radical ideas from the Internet and develop them in their own corner. The EU Commission has then come up with the idea of setting a platform of cooperation between local, national and European authorities. The idea has never really been put into practice.

The deradicalisation programs in prisons are each home made and do not interact on European level.

Then the clash of mentalities kicks in, therefore EU does not stand united against terror.

In the Western Europe, politicians are talking about tolerance and peace, about integrating the Muslim communities and reaching out to the disadvantaged. The migration is not an issue here that can be related to the terrorism phenomenon.

In the East, the tolerance and peace are not taken into account. Migration is an issue and countries like Hungary and Slovakia are convinced that terrorists are coming in Europe disguised as migrants.

Little is there to say to contradict them since two of the Paris attackers did actually enter Europe through Greece with fake Syrian passports and were picked up in Hungary by a third attacker.

The East will not help the West. As long as the West stubborn to remain tolerant, the East wants nothing to do with it. Also, the Eastern and Central Europe has only been indirectly hit by terrorism, no attacks have yet been perpetrated in Hungary, Poland, Romania or Slovakia.

They think that France, UK, Germany and even Spain deserve to be punished not only for their tolerance, but also for their colonial past.

Then talk about unity. Which real unity can there be when the Western nations, although hit by the same catastrophe, they all have different ways of reacting to it? It's cultural and it's nobody's fault. You just cannot compare the way the French will deal with grief, anger and fear to the British way of dealing with the same thing.

Take Paris and Manchester attacks, for example. They both occurred during musical events gathering lots of people.

In Paris, the Bataclan opened again a year afterwards and in order to mark the event, another concert was organised. No French artist was available for the occasion and nobody was willing to go on stage. The Eagles of Death Metal, who were in concert that dreadful night of the attacks, were not welcomed anymore by the owners of Bataclan. The English singer Sting did it in the end just to help out, although he had nothing to do with the events.

In Manchester, the American singer Ariana Grande pulled herself together after the attack which killed a great number of her fans and did the show again after two weeks. The event was huge and Ariana brought most of her friends with her on stage.

This Anglo-Saxon resolve and unity against fear was more credible one than all the memorial plaques the French and Belgians have put on display after each attack.

When one of the performers shouted to the thousands of young people attending this second concert *"You are young and you want to have fun! Don't ever let them take this away from you!"*, I really believed him. It meant more than all politicians' statements put together.

And this was a charitable event, the money went to the victims. This did not happen in Paris or in Brussels, for that matter. No unity was shown, no solidarity and the victims, more or less assisted by the national authorities, received very little from charity.

Manchester has united. In the days that followed the attack, huge queues formed outside the tattoo shops in the city, everyone wanted a tattoo of the iconic bee. The money went to charity.

And let's talk about the victims of all these attacks, the ones that we so quickly forget once the event is not in the news anymore.

The national legislations do not envisage the compensation for the foreign victims injured in an attack. They do not cover their nationals if they are injured abroad.

In Belgium today, more than a year after the Brussels attacks, one American victim still lies in an hospital bed. Her expenses aren't covered by anyone except her family and friends. The legislation is said to be changing soon, but how soon?

We are all in the same boat, but not for the same reasons

So can we be willing to help each other out?

We often tend to forget why this EU or better yet the European Communities were ever created. How come all these nations that apparently had nothing in common, except religion and sometimes language, have decided to unite?

The brilliant idea belonged to Robert Schuman, a Luxembourgish whose father was French of Luxembourgish language and whose mother was Luxembourgish, but acquired German citizenship after marriage. Schuman had, in his personal history, the very essence of the EU, born under French and German auspices.

In the core of 1950 Europe, people were starving and coping with the loses of war. Together, they built a utopia: nations formerly at war, became friends, partners and holders of values like peace, democracy and solidarity.

Later, in the seventies and eighties and up to the middle of the nineties other nations joined. They were all more or less committed to the principle values that Schuman brought forward in the fifties.

All that changed when people started being hungry again; when the crisis hit the EU and many jobs were lost while others were not created, when the youth unemployment reached record levels, even the true at heart Europeans started to ask themselves: why was the EU even there?

I don't know whether the politicians responsible for the EU realised from 2010 onwards that the EU is just not able to solve the today crisis. It lacks the proper legislation (which is sometime improved on the way), it lacks the vision and the political will.

And let's take a look at the former communist countries. When the Central and Eastern Europeans joined in 2004, 2007 and 2013 they were not impressed by European values.

These were nations that never belonged to the *"western"* club. With the exception of Poland, they had not been affected in the same way as the West by the WWII and could not compare their stories with those of France or the UK. Some of them fought in the German camp during the 40's.

They all had the plague of communism which scarred them for the eternity. They were remorseful and had mixed feelings towards the West and particularly towards Germany.

They asked to be paid for their sufferings which lasted long after the war.

Poland made Germany pay not only for the 1939 invasion, but for all the communism wrong doing that followed after 1945. Hungary wanted the recognition of having been the small county that single-handed rejected the Russian invasion in the 1950's and continued to fight communism afterwards. The recognition was better expressed with money.

The Baltic Republics, fresh from their separation from USSR, had their accounts to settle too with the big powers. Czechs and Slovaks, being small countries, have relied on Germany to pull them through the transition after the communism and the Velvet Revolution.

Romania and Bulgaria missed their start in the EU accession talks in 2000 and had to wait and extra year. Their story is different. They were both former German allies; Bulgaria lost the war while Romania turned against Berlin in that dreadful summer of 1944. This led to the Russian invasion and the creation of a Russian-led government in less than a day.

Due to their geographical position, their entanglement with Moscow and the orthodox faith, they had been, by far, the two countries the most affected by communism.

In their talks with the EU, they were casted as unreliable and corrupted and today still they have to prove their European faith. But they are happy with money that the pre accession and the accession process brought in.

The Eastern European countries have not joined the Union for its shared values and not even for the peace prospects. At the time, back in 2004 and 2007 and even in 2013, the Russian expansion was a remote threat.

They joined in for the tangible benefits: money and the common market.

It took a while to the naïve western politicians to understand their new partners. It wasn't their fault.

This is best reflected in an incident that occurred the 18th of June 2005 when EU 25 was battling for the next seven years EU budget agreement.

A deal was not within reach and the then EU Luxembourg Presidency had held difficult overnight talks during a EU summit in Brussels.

It then emerged, first as a rumour, then as a confirmed story told by the then Luxembourg's Prime Minister Jean-Claude Juncker, that the new member states had stood up one after another offering to give up funds they had been offered, in the interests of reaching an agreement.

"I am sad and ashamed," Junker told the press with tears of bitterness in his eyes.

I was in that crowd of journalists that day and I felt sorry for him. At some point I was even close of asking for the microphone and state a very unusual question: *"Don't you see, Prime Minister, that this is all a ruse ???"* Up to this day, I'm still sorry I didn't do it.

Politicians like Juncker, old fashion, true in their hearts, passionate Europeans, children of the war, could not see the truth about their eastern counterparts.

In the aftermath of the big enlargement in 2004, when eight formerly communist countries joined, the mirage of the European unity was glowing.

They brought with them Cyprus and Malta that agreed to join for reasons of closer ties with the continent. The divided Cyprus was there in a hope of unity with their lost northern half. This has not yet happened, 13 years after Cyprus joined the EU.

"A reunited continent!" That was the slogan of the big enlargement and we cannot argue with that: the continent no longer had a dividing wall or an iron curtain.

But was Europe ever united, even before the wars or the Russian invasion in the East?

In 2004, the moment of the greater ever expansion of the EU could have been poetical, if only what the poets said was true.

Ninety years after the break of the WWI, that destroyed the European empires, but created new countries instead, Europe was finally reunited. Politicians and media alike spread the slogan, but in the East it didn't take.

The reluctance the East Europeans came from a simple fact: the pre 1914 Europe was not united at all.

And even after the disappearance of the Prussian and Ottoman empires and the decline of the British domination, Europe was still a sad place.

It took another war, the most vicious and unforgivable act of cruelty of man against man, in order for the continent to be shaped again. For the worse.

The Eastern European nations have understood that during their 50 years of imprisonment in the Russian camp. They are not easily fooled and don't get impressed by poetic phrases. They want the money and the tangible benefits, like the free travel and to secure jobs in Brussels.

It is therefore easy to see why the word *"solidarity"* means so little to us European today.

Between the many crisis and the lack of common goals, the Europeans of today cannot help and will not help each other out.

And for the Eastern bloc, as stated above, the word *"solidarity"* lost all its meaning during those times when they were gazing at an empty sky waiting for the American planes to come and save them. The Americans never came for them, but the Russians did. Funny enough, even back in the fifties, the Eastern European never expected their Western brothers to help out.

So how can they be expected to show solidarity and kindness when it comes to take in refugees from Syria and ease the burden on Italy and Greece?

It is sad and infuriating, but Hungary, Slovakia, Poland and Romania said *"no"* to that solidarity which was expected from them. They were the truthful ones, the ones who did not pretend to care. Others, in Northern part of Europe, said *"yes"*, but did little or nothing.

Romania played it wisely, for once; Bucharest said *"no"* to the relocation system of refugees, but only to the system; it did take in some refugees and escaped Brussels' anger.

The other three countries said *"no"* and they meant it, even if that triggered sanctions from the EU Commission and eventually a legal action as well. Unimpressed by the Juncker's wrath, Hungary and Slovakia brought EU Commission to Court, before being themselves sued by Brussels.

But today's politicians in the Western world fail to understand why people miss out on solidarity.

It is not only the migration phenomenon that brought anger into people's hearts. The Greek crisis, the bank crisis, the wave of terrorism across western world and the lack of efficient response form EU's side, all these contributed to the today's lack of human compassion and the rise of the extreme right.

Young Europeans to the rescue!

A happy future of the EU should rely on the young and the restless, but the EU has failed them spectacularly.

It may seem harsh or even unjust to say that the EU has given up on the young, but this is the truth.

The Youth Strategy, launched in 2010 and funded by the member states (€6 billion were granted to it), has died since. It was supposed to bring new employment and education opportunities, but the capitals have not implemented it.

Yet again we see that the EU Institutions are not entirely to be blamed when things go wrong or when solutions don't work. The member states do a lot of harm too.

The issue was in the news when an unprecedented high level of unemployment among the young was reported in 2010 mainly in Spain, Portugal and Greece, but France was not too proud either. It was also heavily used in the 2014 campaign for the European elections. But since it was a campaign issue, it stayed there and did not develop beyond.

The EU Commission came to the rescue and proposed this Youth Strategy which was warmheartedly adopted then by the MEPs and the EU leaders.

The last report issued by the EU Commission was in October 2015. The next one, if any, will be in 2018. But on national level, almost nothing has been done. The issue was scraped from the priorities and we simply do not talk about it anymore.

So how do the young feel? Well, depends whom we are talking about.

The ones that were looking for a job and were in their early twenties in 2010 are not considered *"young"* any more, whether they have since found a job or not.

The young of today are not even aware that the EU once had a youth strategy. Some of them are aware of another publicity stunt that the EU has launched prior to 2010, the bank loans for the young.

It was merely an invitation addressed to the banks to be more flexible on loans for the young who wanted to start a professional life. It didn't take, the banks did not see it that way. They have established across Europe their own, different and less attractive offers for young entrepreneurs and some of them have targeted offers for the young farmers.

In 2011, EU Commission also proposed a European Loan Guarantee Facility for Erasmus Master students. This was slammed by the European Student's Union which considered it harmful for the young.

Their reaction seemed odd, but they might have had a point. The Student's Union said that this was a way to help the banks, not the young and was concerned about the potential brain drain impact that this type of loan might have had. The Commission was also aware of this and of the disparities among regions in terms of access to higher education, but failed to address the issue.

The Commission also fuelled another project, Erasmus Plus, an upgraded version of the university exchange programme Erasmus, which still benefits from over €2 million per year.

It has grouped other previously existing programmes and it's now a big thing, but some of its parts, like Erasmus for traineeships, are difficult to implement.

All in all, some of the EU projects worked, some didn't, the youth unemployment dropped from 25% in 2010 to 16,9% in 2017, but the young are still left out in the cold.

Nevertheless, some young European are enthusiastic about Europe and this happens mainly in the Central and Eastern Europe.

Look at the enthusiasm shown during the political gatherings the young have in the East and you'll see I'm right.

In the East, the generation of those born after 1990 is now is the prime of its life. They did not live through the communism and the transition was beneficial for them. Their parents had hard lives, but they don't know about it. Some of them who do know of the older times are glad to have had such a narrow escape.

They are young, restless and they hold dear values like democracy and freedom in countries that did not always observe these values closely.

Just recently young Romanians took it to the streets when different governments have praised corruption, restricted the freedom of the press and the independence of the judiciary. Young Hungarians defended in big rallies the Central European University and young Polish challenged the right wing government when it endangered the rule of law.

These people are proud to be seen peacefully demonstrating and clearly stating what they believe in. They know that "*Europe*" sees them doing the right thing, being true Europeans. These are spontaneous demonstration, true citizen's response to corrupted and ill-intentioned actions of politicians.

In the Western part of the continent, rallies are organised by the Unions. Either they are against the pensions' reform or one tax or another, Unions organise these big rallies and almost all them take place in Brussels. There's something irritating about this, something untrue: this is not the people's voice, this is one doubtful power struggling with another doubtful power.

Therefore, I was amused when questioned by a French journalist about the huge rallies of the young that took place in Bucharest in January 2017. She thought that the rallies were organised by some union or another. When I told her that this was not the case, she seemed puzzled. Well, I said to myself, I can't blame her, the last time the young took it to the streets in Paris by their own force was in 1986 or even 1960, both events ending up with the occupation of Sorbonne.

The post 1990 Eastern Europe has awoken to private ownership. Many of these young people's parents are owners of a shop or of a business. The young can follow into their parents' steps or, if they choose a different path of life, they know they can always have a job secured for them in the family business.

For those of them whose parents are in the academic world it is still a thrill to have careers alike. The son of a teacher or academic will probably try and live up to the standards seen in the family.

The situation is different in the rural area, of course, that is to be expected anywhere in the world.

Most of the young in the East speak high-level English, have studied and travelled abroad and became convinced by the European values. For them, the EU means mobility, studies, fun and sometimes jobs.

There are those who choose to leave their countries of birth and to settle in France, in Belgium, even in the UK or elsewhere. Most of these are Romanians or Polish, sometimes Hungarian.

And the EU job part was easy for East Europeans since more than ten years after the big enlargement, the institutions in Brussels, Luxembourg and Strasbourg had to fill-in their national quotas for newcomers.

Starting in 2004 and up to 2015 even, the EU competitions were meant to bring in civil servants from the East on permanent and temporary bases, on all grades and capacities.

Meanwhile, the French, the Germans, the Belgians or the British were rarely permitted to enter those competitions.

A French friend who was trying in vain to get a job with the EU Commission once told me with some resentment: *"Tu devras le faire, tu as la bonne nationalité."*

She eventually got an under qualified job and she tried endlessly to pass to an upper level. She let go her anger once by saying *"Y'a tous ces crétins de l'est qu'on traite comme de rois!"* In the end, she was told that she had to learn Romanian or Polish in order to secure her position. She left the EU Commission soon afterwards.

Oh, yes! In the west, things don't look so bright. Here, the young are often as qualified as their Eastern generation mates, but they are less prepared for life.

Their parents have lived rich full lives. They swung through the 1970's and 1980's without a trace of worry. They only came to realise that the good times are over after the year 2000. The western market of jobs and services collapsed after the 2001 attacks against USA.

Their sons and daughters can no longer have the nice life they had. No job, no money, no foreign languages duly taught in school, no diploma or too many diplomas: these youngsters are not fit to struggle in today's world.

A middle-aged Belgian policewoman once told me that she had come to realise that, unlike her parents, she won't be able to retire while still young and live a happy retirement in South of France or in Spain. She also realised that she could not help her children buy their first house or apartment and she will probably not have a peaceful old age.

The young from the West are also the beneficiaries of studying abroad through Erasmus and other EU funded programs, but when that's all over, the reality kicks in.

The importance of holding a diploma or at least a degree is less and less tangible in the West nowadays, although various studies have shown that the probability of unemployment is bigger in the absence of proper training.

Unlike the Eastern world, the West is now suffocating the private business through taxes and regulations. More and more private–owned companies in all sectors of activity are due to shut down or to reluctantly agree to a takeover. The parents of these young are less and less in position to offer them a cosy place in the family business.

Therefore, the Western world is not on the mending, since the young have deserted it.

The relooking of France after the young Emmanuel Macron became president in May 2017 is a thread of hope for the young. Old politicians and parties have had a massive defeat during the presidential elections. A new wave of youth and renewal has swiped through France, but is this all for real?

The young French look at it in disbelief. Three out of four young French did not vote for the parliamentary elections in June 2017.

All over Western Europe the young are trying to make the difference between right and wrong. Their susceptible minds are put at risk by the rise of the extreme right speeches and the collapse of the job market.

The Brexit dilemma

Brussels woke up that morning of 24th of June 2016 to find out that it has lost the UK.

In the EU Commission corridors in Berlaymont building, a British civil servant was looking for the elevator. Two of his colleagues, a French and a Pole who were passing by, maliciously asked him whether he had already cleaned his desk or whether he needed help with that.

More emotion followed as none other than the President of the institution, Jean-Claude Juncker, stated at noon that he wanted the UK out as soon as possible. He was followed by the German chancellor Angela Merkel who, more pragmatically, asked the UK to quickly settle its leave as not to upset the financial markets any further.

Was this a nightmare or was it for real? Juncker came down to the press room in one of his very rare encounters with the media in these premises. He had tears in his eyes and he was not the only one crying.

Some of the British journalists accredited in Brussels, the same that had criticised Europe for years and praised London's will to get out of the project, were crying too.

None of us has yet woken up from this nightmare. But how did the EU allow that to happen? We all know about the campaign of the Brexiters and how little truth was in that.

We know (or we should know) that the EU could not get involved in this campaign. It kept out because there are no rules that allow the EU to get involved in the private domestic affairs of its member states.

But how come a state can leave the EU, why is it even possible?

Escaping from Paradise

At the very beginning, the EU was conceived as an open club which demanded the respect of the fundamental values as an entry ticket. But there was a catch: once a country entered the club, it was not permitted to leave it.

Nobody forced anyone to stay, the question was not even raised. But nothing in the Treaties specified that there could be a way out of the club.

And why should it? This was a Paradise on Earth that promised peace and prosperity, unity and solidarity. Except it wasn't, not for everyone.

More than a hundred years ago, Oscar Wilde said that America was a paradise from which women are trying to escape. Maybe this was to be applied to the EU too. Maybe, at some point, an exit clause had to be envisaged.

And envisaged it was, only none of those who sat down and thought of it actually meant it for real.

Let's go back a few years and place ourselves in their position.

Previous to the projected success of the 2004 enlargement, EU was so full of itself that it couldn't imagine anything may one day go wrong.

It actually went so well, that the EU also wanted to have a Constitution that will give it a political figure for its people and the world. The common market, the free trade zone, was no longer enough for this wonderful construction that "united" Europe.

This Constitution was later downgraded to a Treaty and that Treaty contains a tricky article: the article 50...

The *"exit close"* of article 50 was there for spite: *"Let's see who dares to leave the EU!"*. It was also a pretended sign of flexibility that meant to say *"EU is not a prison"*. Between these mixed signals given by article 50, the Brussels-based eurocrats never thought that it will come to a country actually wanting to leave the EU.

And the irony goes on: the article 50 was drawn up by a British diplomat, John Kerr, who recently stated: *"I didn't have UK in mind"*.

Back in 2003, after much deliberation (the costly and ineffective European Convention that brought together politicians and civil society during many months in Brussels), a Constitution was drafted.

So does the EU now have a Constitution? No, it doesn't. The French and the Dutch rejected the idea by referendum in 2005. Their vote was actually not against this text as such, but against all the other things that the Europeans were disagreeing with.

For the Dutch, it was the precisely the big and marvellous enlargement from the year before. For the

French, it was the deterioration of the social rights. The other EU countries did not hold a referendum.

The vote was an early wakeup call about people being disenchanted with the way things were in the EU long before the big crisis even started.

But the European politicians got it all wrong. They didn't realise that people cannot connect to the bureaucratic Europe, the one imposing directives, norms and regulations.

Although all these are meant to improve business climate, economy growth, food security, people welfare and animal well-being, they are applied in such way that people feel persecuted by Brussels.

Politicians thought that this was all about communicating Europe and therefore tried to communicate better.

There was some truth in that and it could've worked if the communication had really improved. But all they did, in the end, is that they invented EU funded media projects that were supposed to bring the citizens closer.

The radio network, EURANET (later upgraded to EURANET PLUS) was created in a number of member states with the aim of bringing tailored information from Brussels to the most remote communities of this Europe. The money came from Brussels.

Press EU, a press review translating articles from all across Europe into several languages was also created.

Both projects are now dead.

"The British should've never joined

...but now, since they are in, they should stay in"
These words of wisdom were spoken by a young man who was answering a question of a journalist, in the streets of Marseille, in the aftermath of the Brexit vote.

Since the end of the sixties and up to today, the French have kept their doubts about the British and vice-versa.

When the labour Prime Minister Harold Wilson, in the 1963, first thought about joining the club set up in Brussels, he did it for economic reasons.

The then French President Charles De Gaulle didn't even consider his request. De Gaulle thought the British were unreliable and not true Europeans.

"England in effect is insular, she is maritime, she is linked through her interactions, her markets and her supply lines to the most diverse and often the most distant countries; she pursues essentially industrial and commercial activities, and only slight agricultural ones.

She has, in all her doings, very marked and very original habits and traditions. »

This was De Gaulle's thinking. Ten years later, when France's De Gaulle had left power and a more flexible Georges Pompidou had taken his place, UK stood another chance.

It was the Tory Prime Minister Ted Heath who brought London to the Brussels table and a fine job he did too. In the beginning of the eighties, Margaret Thatcher, the first female British Prime Minister, found that the ties with Brussels were harmful for Britain.

During those times, nobody dared questioning the European construction led by the French and merely financed by Germany.

Thatcher was not impressed by the French and their dominant attitude. She thought Britain was misled into paying too much for the welfare of the French farmers. She said Britain had lost a great deal in joining the EEC as it did and renegotiated the British contribution to Brussels.

"It is not asking the Community for money, it is asking the community to have our own money back!", she said.

Don't forget these were times when countries like France and Germany had an economic boost, while the UK, against the background of industrial decline and social unrest, was *"the sick man of Europe"*.

This led to the *"British rebate"* which still exists and reduces by more or less 66% the net contribution of Britain to the EU budget.

But at no point Thatcher thought about leaving the club. On the contrary. In an odd and surprising way, Thatcher felt at home in that European construction that was rapidly developing.

During the 1980's, UK brought new ideas and new challenges into the club. Brussels already had a policy regarding undeveloped regions and countries and took a lot of pride in it.

We were mainly speaking, at the time, about former French and Dutch colonies in Africa and in the East. Britain has brought in a new approach for external development as it added to the list of European priorities India and the entire Commonwealth.

Britain has kept its former empire ways of dealing with the world. British diplomats and high level civil servants have contributed to the pragmatic way in which, sometimes, things are still done in the today's Europe.

London has pushed for the fall of the Berlin wall. It was the joint action taken by Margaret Thatcher and the US President Ronald Reagan that brought the wall down. In the aftermath of the communism decline, UK did not oppose to the German reunification and the integration of a stronger

Germany in NATO. France was the one opposing to it.

During those years, UK was different from all others countries of the club. It was original, sparkling, elegant, pragmatic and dominant in a fashionable way.

But De Gaulle was right. The country has kept its insular attitude and opted-out on issues which were thought too communitarian, like the euro and the Schengen agreements.

In 1990, when the EU first started to think of a new and more centralised and structured way in which to operate, Thatcher brutally dismiss the plans.

Her statement in the House of Commons responding to EU Commission President Jacques Delors prompted the Conservatives to ouster Thatcher from 10 Downing Street.

"The President of the Commission, Mr. Delors, said at a press conference the other day that he wanted the European Parliament to be the democratic body of the Community, he wanted the Commission to be the Executive and he wanted the Council of Ministers to be the Senate. No. No. No."

Thatcher had to leave power partly because of her growing and bluntly disapproval of Brussels. Oddly enough, sixteen years later, Britain chose to leave the EU for exactly the same reason exposed by Thatcher in 1990.

London thought that Thatcher manners did not help Britain on EU level. She left power so Britain continued to cooperate with Brussels, but also continued to be reluctant to the EU's plans, even when it didn't quiet openly admitted so.

In 1991 every leader in the EU was in favour of more power in the external policy of the bloc, a more integrated common market and the single currency.

UK's John Major was in Maastricht for the signing of the Treaty that brought all these things to Europe. But as much as he wanted UK to be at the core of the European bloc, he did all he could to stop the euro.

Major was listening, among others, to the voice of the British people who wanted to have nothing in common to this kind of Europe.

This did not exclude Britain from the core of the EU and did not prevent it from becoming one of the most important countries in the club, after Germany and France.

Britain held the exact position it always aimed for and under the strict conditions that it chose for itself.

The French always detested this British attitude towards the European Union and have tried, over the years, to trick London into projects like the single currency (the euro) and the European defence.

And since UK has decided to leave, the EU feels now free to do whatever it always wanted, like a child left home alone. Or so it seems…

EU plans accelerated by Brexit?

In the couple of months that followed the Brexit formal notice (the triggering of article 50 by Prime Minister Theresa May on 29 March 2017), the EU took some important decisions and it did it faster than ever.

The June EU summit was full of nice surprises: plans for a better funded European defence were agreed in ten minutes, the same went for the update of the situation on the relocation of migrants.

This was unprecedented for a EU summit and some saw in that a new beginning for the bloc: ambitious decisions, bigger than never before, carefully planned and taken at the highest level without the usual drama.

Brussels is now nurturing a dream:

Brexit has freed us for finally setting up plans for a European defence; it also freed us for a better integrated, two speeded Eurozone. It gave the EU the possibility of properly thinking of the way ahead without any possible breaks or reluctance from London.

London is out and leaves behind it a more determined, better equipped and more glamorous European Union, led by a strong Merkel-Macron couple, or M&M, if you prefer.

Well, it is now too early to say whether all this holds water.

It may be that Brexit was a good pretext for the European defence plans to go ahead, but it may also be that the Trump administration actually woke up these plans. Since 1998 (the Saint Malo summit), the EU has been thinking of having parallel defence structures, not necessarily competing with NATO.

It was never to be as such, partially because UK had blocked the decision up to 2008 when the joint French and British command was established in Norfolk. Afterwards, during the crisis years, the EU simply couldn't and wouldn't pay for anything at all.

But when Donald Trump started making it clear that the US will no longer finance the defence of the old continent and he clearly demanded all European members of NATO to higher their contribution, something had to be done. The moment was Spring 2017, same time as Brexit notification.

The Europeans thought: what about investing in our own capabilities? It probably would've been done even if the UK was still on board.

The Eurozone greater integration is a German idea and London was somewhat irritated by it. But a deal was struck in February 2016 with the then Prime Minister David Cameron and it specified that the plans could go on in permanent consultation with the City.

82

The deal is off now since it was only available in case of no Brexit, but the plan could have been possible even if UK was still on board.

So the dream of being better off without the Brits may be one that will never come true.

We are all of us going to be weaker and shaken by Brexit and we are all of us responsible for this sad outcome, politicians and media alike. Some did too much, some did too little, some let others do wrong.

In the end of the day, when the divorce is over, none of us is going to be happy.

UK without the EU

The divorce is going to be an ugly one.

Britain plays tough on Brexit, but the EU plays tough as well. *"First people, then money"* is the motto of the EU's negotiator for Brexit, Michel Barnier.

The deal offered by Brussels is simple: first we secure the rights of our citizens living in the UK, then we can discuss whether London should still be part of the internal market after Brexit.

The problem is Britain says it no longer cares for the internal market and wants out; this is what in EU jargon is called *"hard Brexit"*.

So what is there to negotiate? The money! Brussels thinks of presenting London with the bill for Brexit which could be as high as €100 billion. EU wants the money to be paid in its single currency and not in pounds, because the Pound is seen as too volatile nowadays.

The bill is actually the addition of the sums of money UK still needs to pay to the EU budget and for the financing of EU external commitments up to the date of the actual divorce. Some negotiation is possible around these figures, but there is not much room left on either side to lower or to higher *"the fine"*.

And Britain is not making concessions. Brussels wanted a secure status for EU citizens living in the UK, London has offered anything but…

In the offer made public by the British government on 26th of June 2017, EU citizens in Britain are offered the possibility of applying for residence status, but the terms are not clear to Brussels.

The proposal was practically dismissed by different EU actors, among which Angela Merkel who put it bluntly: *"It seems that the four freedoms of the EU are not respected, we'll have to act according to that"*.

In other words: *"this is going to be a very unpleasant fight"*.

The nature of the Brexit will define the future of all Europeans.

The hard Brexit will lead to London leaving the EU internal market, to commercial barriers and higher prices on imports and exports, lost jobs and lost trade opportunities.

It will also lead to Britain securing trade ties elsewhere, without being tied up by the EU rules. Brussels looks to these British plans in disbelieve.

But there are business opportunities for UK as a stand-alone country, especially in the East. Japan and China are willing to talk business with London and that infuriates Brussels which nevertheless claims that UK has no good negotiators and will never accomplish anything in this respect.

When UK first hinted to the possibility of a *"golden era"* agreement with China, in February 2017, Jean-Claude Juncker was furious!

"Trade deals are the remit of the EU... Britain cannot complete trade deals with half the world—although it is doing the opposite," he said.

In the same time, the EU was doing its bid on an agreement with Japan. Concrete steps have been achieved so far, but Japan wants to hold early free trade talks with Britain too, amid growing concern over post-Brexit access to the European market.

Therefore, to put it in the words of Homer Simpson, we might ask ourselves: *"who's stupid now? "*

Bad English, "*français aproximatif* "or…

…better yet, German! Which is the language that will prevail in Brussels?

For many, Brexit rimes with the loss of the dominance of the English language in the Brussels bubble.

Wrong! EU has 23 official languages and three of them are working languages: English, French and German.

English will remain an official and a working language after Brexit (sorry, guys) because it is one of Malta's speaking languages. If Malta decides to withdraw English from the EU's billboard, then it should plead with the EU member states for that. Their decision must be taken by unanimity.

Of the three working languages, English is the most spoken one and all documents of the bubble are written in English and translated (if needed) into (all) other languages. All EU civil servants, journalists, lobbyists, caterers, landlords, pub owners, even the cleaning ladies speak English.

French and German are also spread, but much less.

But don't imagine that the English language spoken in Brussels is the one you were taught in school and you'll practice in London. And for the native speakers the shock is going to be important.

The Brussels English is *"bad English"*, as a French colleague of mine once explained to a group of Romanian journalists visiting the bubble.

It is jargon English, a language invented in Brussels where some words from the English language may appear, but all others are just gibberish.

"Phasing in", *"phasing out"*, *"top up"* (terms related to EU money), *"emergency brake"* (expression related to the freedom of movement), *"the six-pack and the two-pack agreements"* (no, it's not beer, it's banking union), all these are to be found in the documents written in the bubble.

Nobody knows for sure where they came from or which civil servant has invented the one or the other. They go into the language quicker than light and they stay there. Journalists adopt them and they cross to other languages, much to the French despair.

The Eastern bloc of mostly English speaking countries almost never translate *"infringement"* into Bulgarian, Hungarian or Romanian. The term is taken as such.

Some of the French journalists try to find a French term for every invention from Brussels, but they don't always succeed.

The French have a real issue with the dominating English.

Most of the accredited French journalists in Brussels don't speak proper English and they feel frustrated in many occasions when they deal with EU civil servants. The French language dominance in the institutions and among the accredited press has decreased by so much that there is almost impossible nowadays to write an email in French and get a reply in the same language.

I was criticised more than once that I don't impose the French language on EU civil servants especially since I represent the French media. I don't really think I deserve the criticism. When I write an email or pick up the phone, I do it in order to receive prompt information. I do so by speaking/writing in English, being good or bad.

There are rules about the use of the languages, but practically nobody follows those rules today.

For instance, in the EU Commission's press room, a question asked in one of the three working languages should be replied in the same language.

Journalist basically use French and English. Most of the questions addressed in French will be replied to in English or in such bad French that the answer is almost impossible to understand.

On Wednesdays, when EU Commissioners come down to the press room, they do their bid in English, then answer questions in English (with the exception of The President Jean-Claude Juncker who also addresses the press in German, beside French and English, Commissioner Gunther Oettinger who speaks frequently German and the First Vice President Frans Timmermans who could fluently speak six languages, including Italian and Dutch).

All the rest will speak incredibly bad English with such a disturbing accent that you'll pray that would speak Latvian or Slovak instead.

The most comical one is the ambitious French Commissioner Pierre Moscovici who manages (after two years in the office) to be fluent in English but he kept his French accent to such an extent that he is almost impossible to follow.

But the award of the most embarrassing on the job must go to Michel Barnier, the very EU's Brexit negotiator who tries to speak English (his efforts go back to 1999) but never succeeds. He then reads phrases written for him by his team without always understanding their meaning. When he gets to the questions from the British media, he has the translation in one ear and he replies in French, most of the time.

So what's going to happen after Brexit? Will French prevail over English? Will German be replacing the two? Well, I'll stick to the wisdom of my French colleague and say: "*Nay, we're going to be still speaking bad English*".

We are all in the gutter...

...**B**ut some of us are looking at the stars? I apologize for adding the question mark Mr Oscar Wilde's famous quote, but when it comes to the EU, the doubt seems reasonable.

The presidents of two crucial EU institutions clashed like a couple of kids in July 2017 when most of the MEPs failed to attend a debate in Strasbourg. The debate was regarding the outcome of the Maltese EU Presidency, marked by little achievement and one little corruption scandal involving the Prime Minister.

Business as usual, you'd say, but Jean-Claude Juncker said that the EU Parliament was *"ridiculous"*. Antonio Tajani rejected the criticism and asked him to rephrase it. Juncker persisted in calling MEPs ridiculous and words continued.

The incident was a field trip for the press and added salt and pepper to the plenary, but it was actually a sad display of mistrust and poor cooperation.

Imagine, this happened when the Brexit talks had just begun amid claims of unity and bravery from the EU's side! Some unity they both showed there, Tajani and Juncker, when they jumped at each other's throats!

It is widely known that Juncker was working better with the former EU Parliament President, Martin Schulz. Tajani was elected after three rounds of votes in the winter of 2016 in another sad display, this time one of power grapping.

First, social-democrat Schulz refused to quit his post after already five years on the job.

Schulz was supposed to have left the seat to the Christian-democrats that had put forward Tajani, but instead he clung to the position and was eventually kicked out.

Then, once he left, his social-democrats fellows refused to leave the top seat to Tajani, so a vote had to be organised.

Juncker was unhappy to lose Schulz and even unhappier to gain Tajani. And it showed.

When Juncker called the MEPs' house *"ridiculous"*, he also threatened never to return again, which would be a serious disruption in the EU decision making process.

Well, the truth has it that the MEPs are really disrespectful to their guests and that the presence of the Maltese Prime Minister that morning in the chamber was a compulsory one. He had to be there, the MEPs had to be there too.

So this is how the EU institutions cooperate on the verge of Brexit. Let's take a look at the member states now.

Austria announced also in July that it intends to defend its border with Italy against migration. Italy was shocked by the news and has summoned the Austrian ambassador in Rome.

Croatia still refuses to recognize the arbitration judgment in its maritime dispute with Slovenia, with police boats that play to mark their territory at sea.

In the meantime, East clashed with the West over the *"posted workers"*. Brussels clashed with Warsaw and Budapest over the rule of law. Warsaw took the matter to a personal level and started attacking not so much the EU Commission, but one EU Commissioner particularly: Frans Timmermans.

So who's looking at the stars?

Well, I guess that some of us do when we are not involved in politics or decision making. Making a better future for the children, having a bigger house or a stable employment, these are all dreams that sometimes come true.

And, believe or not, some EU political and practical ideas are aiming for a better Europe.

All in all, people do not entirely realize what is done for them or to them. Nevertheless, their opinion is sometime required.

Let the people decide?

Take a look at Belgium, the bizarre little kingdom placed in the heart of Europe, home to most of the EU Institutions and NATO headquarters. Belgians are not glamorous and they don't claim being as smart as their neighbours. But, in a way, they are…

Belgium has banned the referenda a hundred years ago when it realized that whatever it did, the Flemish vote will have it as the Flemish are more numerous than the Walloons.

Other countries in Europe are still believing (or pretending to believe) that the people's voice should be heard when it comes to political matters.

Nowadays, so many referendums have failed to confirm the will of the top politics that one can only think that sometimes, if you want a project to fail, you must ask the people to vote on it.

And when a project fails through referendum, the politicians are still imposing it on people.

The Maastricht treaty referendum about the introduction of the euro has almost failed in France in 1992. Half of the French who voted were against the project, but they use euro nowadays.

Another referendum organized in 2005 in France, and this time in The Netherlands too, has denied Europe the dream of having a Constitution. But the French and the Dutch are living today in a European Union ruled by a Treaty which took the most parts of the rejected EU Constitution.

The Dutch have rejected in 2016 an Association Agreement between EU and Ukraine. The Dutch government was still forced to find a way around that so the Agreement could enter into force.

If referenda are the way of bringing the people closer to the EU project, so be it! But are they well informed?

People do not read the communication material put out by the EU institutions or by the national governments. People nowadays turn to the social networks almost exclusively.

Since the explosion of the social networks, the information there runs on a freeway with no demarcation lines, no signals and no security at all.

Some of us learn about the political projects of the moment through those chats and get it more or less right.

All of us have come across opinions expressed by people who got it more or less themselves and then passed it on.

So, we read or hear about the ultra-liberal Europe, the fascist or even the communist Europe! There are those who criticized the two terms Commission of José Manuel Barroso whose ultra-liberal approach has ruined the Europe's economy.

There are those who, on the contrary, criticized the first ever political EU Commission, the one of Jean-Claude Juncker, for not doing enough to free the economy.

There are those expressing in favour of the free comprehensive trade agreements with Canada, USA or Japan and there are those who think that these are the worst possible scenarios for Europe.

And although the ten years that José Manuel Barroso spent in Brussels as EU Commission President were the years established as a mediocre leadership of Europe, it is actually the Juncker Commission which is the most hated.

Juncker has a so and so team, not too bright and not too dull.

It has some important figures like the First Vice President France Timmermans and the foreign affairs

EU chief Federica Mogherini, but it just doesn't deliver.

Jean-Claude Juncker is in permanent competition with the EU leaders over the political leadership of Europe. He also has an unprecedented challenge to face, the Brexit challenge.

But Juncker is also the first elected President of the EU Commission.

Few people in Europe, besides the EU staff and accredited press in Brussels, realized that the EU Commission President was chosen in a non-transparent manner by the EU leaders until 2014.

That changed once the Lisbon Treaty applied to the 2014 European elections when each political group in the EU Parliament put forward a public candidate for the top EU Commission job. This was called *"a Spitzenkandidat"*, since the exercise was never done before in the EU.

The party that won the most seats, the EPP, has gained the commission job too. The candidates were presented to the voters in Europe via several public debates broadcasted live on Euronews and France 24.

But was Juncker really elected? What has actually changed in 2014?

Well, it is hard to say. He has been a candidate, he was known and participated in public debates, but he actually had the job because the EPP won the European elections.

Prior to 2014, the EU leaders chose the EU Commission President behind closed doors and in secret, but the person chosen was each time representing the political group that had just won the European elections. In sum, nothing has changed.

Jean-Claude Juncker became much more known than his predecessors and also highly controversial, but not because he was the first one to be *"elected"*, but because all the criticism he has been facing.

He is much disliked in Eastern and Central Europe, he's tolerated by France, controlled by Germany and hated by UK.

All in all, the attempt to bring more democracy and transparency into the European process has failed and if one of the key figures is widely known today, that happened for the wrong reasons.

The Spitzenkandidat experiment failed so spectacularly that the political groups in the EU Parliament gave up on trying it again in 2019.

The Visegrad pain in the back

The Visegrad group (Poland, Czech Republic, Slovakia and Hungary) is well known in Brussels as over the years, before and after the 2004 enlargement, it has been constantly standing up for the rights of the Central Europeans.

The group, also called V4, is perceived as a strong voice of the new comers who are defending themselves against the big countries and seeking to get things in their best interest.

So far so good.

They fought together for better deals under the Common Agriculture Policy during their EU Accession and fought again for better funding and regional funds when the current budget framework was negotiated.

But everything went wrong when the migration crisis worsened and when the government in Poland changed, making way for the right wing populist national-conservative Law and Justice Party (PiS).

As previously shown, the EU is not ready to deal with these countries. It doesn't understand them, it doesn't quiet respect them and it always misses the point when negotiating with them.

In addition to that, EU is not equipped to mend broken democracies as this scenario should have never happened. It was all about democracy, values and trust.

Brussels trusted the Greeks with the figures and the Eastern countries with their values. Dead wrong!

And once it has understood its mistake, the EU Commission tried to adapt to that and failed. What happened is that it has invented a *"structured dialogue"* which is one way of straighten up a naughty country without going to the extreme of suspending its voting rights.

Why not trigger the article 7?

The EU has thought about the hypothetical case where a country may go astray and invented the possibility of suspending its voting rights (article 7 of the EU Treaty), but this is too big a punishment for any respectable state. And all EU's member states are respectable states, aren't they?

Well, no, not all of them and now the problem is that while the article 7 is out of reach for the image's sake, something else should be done.

The structured dialogue seemed to be the answer when the EU Commission invented it in 2014.

The principle of the matter is simple: we talk to the country that gives us headaches; we explain which way it should be going. We nevertheless keep the threat alive: if you don't behave, the article 7 is never too far. Therefore, the problem is fixed in no time and the bad publicity is avoided.

Tough luck! The method was used just once and it failed.

When the structured dialogue was established with Poland in March 2016, the country didn't get impressed by any threats and showed no will of talking to Brussels. In more than a year, the dialogue produced nothing.

Poland is now the only EU country facing a suspension of its voting rights because of the attempts made against the democracy and the rule of law.

If the article 7 of the EU Treaty is triggered against it, that will not only be unprecedented, but it will also have major consequences on the EU's already shattered image.

Similar scenarios have been seen in Romania where different governments (especially social democrat governments) played hide and seek with the rule of law and upset Brussels.

But unlike the Polish, the Romanians are less self-confident and any criticism from Brussels is taken quiet seriously. In 2012, the government of social democrat Victor Ponta has done exactly what the Polish government has done in 2017: it undermined the independence of the judiciary and attacked the freedom of the press.

Brussels (Barroso's team) has issued warnings, Barroso even met Ponta and gave him a *"to do"* list: 11 points that were listing the measures for restoring the good respect of the democracy.

Ponta did everything he was told to do and the matter was rapidly forgotten.

When another social-democrat government voted one late night, in January 2017, an emergency bill giving the civil servants the right to steal, Brussels was upset again.

Another prime minister, this time was Sorin Grindeanu, was greeted in Brussels in February after weeks of huge protests organized against the government in all big Romanian cities.

Brussels acknowledged that the peaceful demonstrations have gathered more than a million people. Grindeanu was forced to annul the bill. The problem was not entirely solved; nevertheless a frontal collision with Brussels was avoided.

The Polish government does not recognize any authority in Brussels and is determined to win the fight with what Warsaw perceives as being an imposed EU power.

This is partially because of the Polish pride and partially because of the slow reaction coming from Brussels.

The Polish, no matter which government is in place in Warsaw, have always asked to be recognised as being different, as being better and as being the nation which has had the most suffering during and after the World War II.

Brussels, the EU Commission, has been reluctant in punishing Poland, mainly because it knows that it will not have much support from the EU member states if it does so.

Therefore, after more than a year of trying to debate with Warsaw and received nothing but insults, the EU Commission openly threatened the country. But when it did so, it also knew that this might be an empty threat.

During these particularly harsh times for the Union, the Commission, when seeking the approval of two thirds of the member states on the matter, knows that UK and Hungary will surely vote against.

The drama was avoided at almost the last minute when, two days before the foreseen date of the sanctions, the Polish President vetoed parts of the measures and put everything on somewhat on hold. But the problem is not entirely avoided and more surprises are possible.

The Commission had another option, should the matter would've proceeded. It did envisage opening another procedure of sanctions against Hungary in the same time, thus avoiding Poland and Hungary helping each other out.

Hungary's new education law has sparked criticism in spring 2017 as it may allow the Central European University (financed by George Soros) to be closed. The law is an infringement of several EU liberties (including the right of establishment and the right to higher education), but after repeated warnings from Brussels, it was still in place in July 2017.

In addition to that, Hungary's Viktor Orbán, although he was facing exclusion from the European People's Party (EPP), was still persecuting the press and had closed down the newspaper Nepszabadszag in October 2016.

There are reasons enough for Brussels to go down on Poland and Hungary, hence weakening the Visegrad group.

The third country of the group giving headaches is Slovakia and his social-democrat prime Minister, Robert Fico.

Unlike Orbán, Fico really had his party (SMER) suspended from the Party of European Socialist (PES) in 2015, but still continued to reject EU Commission's plan to relocate the migrants. He said Slovakia will only accept Christian migrants.

The fourth country, the Czech Republic, is mostly known because of his former President Vaclav Klaus who spoke many times against Europe. In 2009, he demanded an opt-out from the Charter of Fundamental Rights.

The current President, Milos Zeman, wanted to organize a leave referendum after the Brexit vote. Czech Republic, like all the other Visegrad countries, is opposing Brussels migrants' relocation system.

The Visegrad are a closed group, sometimes inviting other countries to their meetings, but most of the time playing it exclusively for their own good.

They invited Emmanuel Macron to attend their summit in Budapest, but only because the matter of the posted workers has come to a point of clear divergence.

Romania's Klaus Iohannis was invited too, but purely symbolically because many of the posted workers working in France today are Romanians.

So these are the problems country and by country. Brussels also has problems with them taken as a group.

One of the problems was sparkled by the migration crisis and the relocation system invented by the EU Commission. The relocation was supposed to have eased the burden on the main coastal countries, like Italy and Greece.

The Visegrad countries did not agree with the system and took the EU Commission to Court. Needless to say that they didn't implement the relocation decision which is a European one and therefore is mandatory.

The Commission wisely waited for some time, issued some warnings and in July 2017 announced that it will sue Poland, Hungary and Slovakia. Brussels stands a better chance in Court as those states are clearly in breach of the EU law, while the EU Commission isn't.

Therefore, the legal advisors in Brussels think that the case of Visegrad Group against Brussels should be dismissed.

These are the facts of the case and they present a moderate interest; the bigger issue which is at stake here is the alteration of EU's good image.

The other problem is the food quality in V4 countries; they are stating that the food quality here is less than it should be and demand a change in the EU legislation concerning the safety of food.

Some western governments have dismissed the idea as *"ridiculous"*, but the Slovak Robert Fico came to Brussels late July 2017 and demanded that it should be so. Jean-Claude Juncker said that it will look into the matter and maybe change something.

That *"maybe"* was the last drop for Fico. He interrupted Juncker who was speaking to the press and for the first time ever in Brussels, two politicians almost argued in front of the press.

Just moments before, Juncker had tried to steal the focus from Fico pretending that he had received a call from his wife and checking his phone as the Slovak was about to speak. He then said *"Oh, is Mrs Merkel!"* The joke made Fico looked like a fool standing in front of the microphone, having the floor and yet not being able to impose.

The V4 attempt to spark another controversy through food safety is a laughable one. The food
106

standards are the same all over Europe and if the taste of the same product is different from country to country, that's just market adaptation.

Romanian government, being caught in the desire to also be acknowledged as the V4 is, also questions the food safety, but got caught on its own game. Also, it has failed to attract Brussels attention.

But is V4 really at odds with Brussels, are they really side-lined by the Juncker Commission or is this just a populist speech those leaders chose to adopt?

The answer is not an easy one.

The Juncker Commission has decided mainly in favour of the big member states on a number of issues, like migration or the posted workers. It has allowed protectionism to be put in place across Europe and it has danced to the tune of Germany and France concerning the labour market.

Juncker himself is no longer the naïve politician he was in 2005 when he believed that the Central and Eastern member states are defenceless lambs ready to give up money for the greater good. He saw through them and he merely despises them.

What he actually understood in the meantime is that there is no telling of what the Central and Eastern politicians are capable of in order to attract votes. Much like any other politicians in Europe, they are capable of selling just about anything to their people, only they are doing it in a more vicious and unscrupulous way.

V4 countries sized the opportunity of blaming the EU and they are doing splendidly.

The times are tough, the dangers are big, the EU project is about to die, so EU needs all the unity it can get while negotiating with London an ugly divorce.

More than that, EU is still hoping that UK will change its mind. In the meantime, little unity and solidarity is to be shown.

Juncker has wisely decided to divide and rule over the V4. In an interview with Politico (again?) he stated that he likes Hungary's Viktor Orbán with whom he said he has "*a caring relationship*". The journalist interviewing him added in the article: "*He didn't make the same pledge about Poland, or even mention it*".

Juncker also said that Poland will feel "*more lonely after Brexit*" than Hungary.

So what the EU Commission chief is trying to do is to separate these friends by creating tension between them, hoping to get down on them more easily once unity of the V4 is broken up.

For the witty and mischievous Juncker, this is a pleasant game. But the fact remains that the situation is extremely sad and dangerous.

If cases like Brexit are not only unprecedented, but unthinkable, law suits of members states against

Brussels and vice versa are just as much. The whole project is going to pieces. The Union no longer lives up to its name.

So what is there to be done? Business as usual? Are we going to hear the orchestra playing while the ship is sinking? Well, it seems so…

The big defence plans

It might be an attempt of the EU to lure us, it might be just another publicity stunt for the EU project or it might just be real: EU is planning to build its own defence.

This is not about an army, but about the European defence industry. The proposal came, as always, from the EU Commission and it was swiftly approved by the EU leaders.

This is not the first time we hear about the subject as such, but it's the first time that the subject is treated from the right angle: the Europeans promised to spend more on capabilities.

There is no question now about competing with NATO or claiming they can do everything on their own.

Don't forget that defence still is the exclusive competence of the states and the EU Institutions can only give advice or push on a path or another. The main cooperation is placed among the capitals, with little going on on European level as such.

But the Union has nevertheless come a long way

Twenty years ago, the EU didn't even have a common foreign policy. The Commission was doing its bid, the member states acted separately and it was all a big a mess. The defence was not even on the agenda.

The defence ministers met in Brussels in informal manner, meaning that they could not take decisions. This is still the case today.

So as everyone was doing something on the external front and almost never coordinated, the idea of a single external approach imposed on EU actors.

They invented the job of an EU High Representative for External Action that cumulated two former positions: the EU Commissioner for external action and the EU's representative. The person having this position represents both the EU executive body and the member states.

During the drafting of the EU Constitution, which was supposed to introduce the job, the secretary of the then EU Commissioner for external action, Chris Patten, made a typo.

Instead of writing *"a double hatted person"*, she typed *"a double hated person"* and double hated that was! The first who held this job, Catherine Ashton, was anything but supported by the capitals or Brussels.

A former geography teacher who became a politician and EU commissioner for trade after the resignation of Peter Mandelson in 2008, Lady Ashton was prompted to the glamorous position of EU's foreign affairs in 2009 mostly by chance.

She was Labour and a woman and the Europeans were supposed to elect to that position a social-democrat and maybe a woman. She was the only one available that could not spark a controversy.

So she got the job she knew nothing about and sailed through the Arab Spring and the Maidan Revolution with the precious help of her team.

Some said she grew on the job.

Footage of her preparing to meet the new Serbian president and admitting she doesn't know what he looks like is nonetheless available on YouTube. It is also common knowledge that she didn't keep an apartment in Brussels and took the train back to London whenever possible.

When Hosni Mubarak left power in Egypt one Friday night in 2011, she is said to have been already embarked in a Eurostar to London. Her team had hard time convincing her to step out of the train in order to record a statement in EU Commission premises.

The second one on the job, the more glamorous and more competent Federica Mogherini, a young politician having had a specialisation on Islam, was imposed on Brussels by the President of the Italian Council Matteo Renzi in 2014.

Federica has quickly imposed worldwide as the EU's High Representative but some say she has become less and less glamorous once the international problems of the past two years emerged.

She was also criticised for having burst into tears during a press conference in Amman when she learned about the Brussels terrorist attacks of 22 March 2016. Some saw here a display of weakness and said that terrorism cannot be fought with tears. They are probably forgetting that only the tough ones don't mind to cry in public.

Back to the defence plans, the EU Commission now informs us that *"the lack of cooperation between Member States in the field of defence"* is estimated to cost annually between €25 billion and €100 billion. 80% of procurement and more than 90% of Research and Technology are run on a national basis. Up to 30% of annual defence expenditures could be saved through pooling of procurement.

Over the years, the Europeans tried to explain to the United States that they don't like the way their defence is organized through NATO structures.

It was painful to watch: a continent which did not spend on defence and did not have half of the needed capabilities, who cannot really agree on a common foreign policy and cannot understand its close neighbours, like Russia, all over sudden felt pride in questioning the American choices.

All attempts to build alliances for defence in Europe failed. Since 1999 (the Saint Malo meeting which created the first French-British cooperation) and till recently, various groups of countries, always gravitating around France, tried and failed to launch a project.

In 2008, France and UK stroke yet another deal under the EU's common defence and security policy. Their joint efforts were supposed to fight pirates in the Horn of Africa and they did. Then it faded away.

EU's battle groups were formed around the same time, these being rapidly deployable units of 1500 troops. European troops are now in Mali and Sahel, Kosovo and Somalia.

These and others were all nice and good up to the point where Donald Trump made it clear, during the 2017 NATO Summit, that Europeans should spend more on defence and singled out the only six European countries of NATO which have done that. France, UK and Germany -the bigger states - were not among them.

That was the wake-up call and paired with Brexit, the US reluctance to still pay for Europe's security has woken up some of the Europeans.

"There is a formal EU framework for this in the form of the permanent structured cooperation (PESCO) which covers the areas of defence and security", former Polish Defence Minister Janusz Onyszkiewicz wrote in July 2017. *"Unfortunately, with the UK leaving the EU, this will deprive the European Union of its largest militaries and defence actors."*

"Soft power is not powerful enough", said Jean-Claude Juncker in June 2017 and some analysts saw here a reference made to the EU's failure to have avoided the hybrid war in Ukraine in 2013.

This could be a real push into a new cooperation between capitals on military and security issues. Procurement of weapons and new technologies is envisaged.

Also, more than €5 billion per year could be spent on EU level, by the member states on improved capabilities and research.

"The EU thus becomes one of the most important investors in European military research." Mihnea Motoc, former Romanian Defence Minister and Deputy Head of Political Strategy Centre recently stated. *"The capabilities window will mobilize €200 million by the end of the current financial perspective and €1 billion each year"*, he added.

You probably noticed that Eastern Europeans are quiet involved in these plans and they believe in them, while their Western counterparts do not much comment the issue.

In July 2017, a month after the go ahead of the EU capitals for the project, France's Macron decided to deprive the French army of €4.5 billion.

This is partially because the Russian threat is not perceived in the same way in different parts of Europe.

The only Eastern Europeans reluctant to the project are the Bulgarians whose Prime Minister Boyko Borisov was reportedly a little afraid that this may be a closed club of defence.

The EU conclusions on the subject, adopted late June 2017, state that those that spend less on defence and whose equipment is insufficient or just missing, will have a period to prepare if they want to participate on missions. The Bulgarian Borisov is said to have interpreted this as an arms race.

Needless to say that the proposal of the EU Commission was first seen by some as an *" illusion"*.

Even in the EU Parliament, some voices talking off the record said that this is going to be another magnificent EU plan ending up in drawer in some top EU official office.

But rest assured, if the plan goes ahead, this will probably never lead to the creation of a European army.

What is more, with the UK outside the EU, some of the plans might just not work as they should.

Onyszkiewicz is right in pointing out that if European Defence Industrial Development or European Defence Fund were set up, but without the UK, to what extent a very powerful British defence industry could be a part of these integration process?

Well, former UN official and security adviser Ilana Bel-El recently wrote for the European Leadership Network: *"The change is fundamentally about the EU and its interests: its survival as a prosperous trade, political and security union, and the freedoms it brings, notably the freedom of movement and especially the sustainability of the Schengen Agreement. Moreover, given the chronology of unrest, this issue has become a matter of political survival for politicians across the EU."*

Amen to that!

A two-speed Europe

It was the 1st March 2017 that the EU Commission came up with the proposal of enabling countries who want to move ahead with the EU integration to do so without being concerned with the others.

For personal reasons, I shall remember that day for the rest of my life. This was the day when things started to go wrong for the one I have considered as being my brother during my entire life.

As I was summing up the proposal for RFI that afternoon, I was hoping against hope that he'll be all right. That wasn't to be. Later that night I left for Paris to see him or what was left of him. He died 10 days afterwards.

The two-speed Europe therefore rings a sad note to me and others (for different reasons), but if you stop to consider it, this is not a bad idea.

Some years back, I was giving a presentation of the current affairs of the EU to young journalists from the Balkans during what we considered troubled moments after the big enlargement.

One of them asked me whether I thought that the EU would survive and if so, in what shape. I remember answering without hesitation: "*the EU will have to have two speeds or it will cease to exist*".

I still believe that now. There's nothing wrong with two speeds, as long as the first speed is what it should be.

Don't look at the idea as big nations plotting against small ones, not even as a clash between old and new EU members. The idea of two speed integration, which has been around almost since the creation of the EEC, this time is about the euro.

The plans were put again on the table by Germany and they were not targeting anyone else but France. This was prior to the victory of Emmanuel Macron when Paris was giving mixed signals about its will for deeper EU integration.

Germany wanted a more intense cooperation within the Eurozone and has launched this warning to France: if you're not able to move, I'm going to do it without you.

After the French elections, the tone changed. Angela Merkel told Emmanuel Macron that more action on Eurozone deepening was foreseen after the German elections. The two leaders agreed to cooperate with some countries, but not with all of them.

The idea is not to exclude anybody while not waiting for everybody indefinitely either.

The Luxembourg Prime Minister Xavier Bettel resumed the situation better at the Rome summit late March when he said he would *"rather have a two-speed Europe than a dead-end and no speed"* Europe. *"When a country says 'I don't want to,' I can say: 'Well, too bad. Don't block me. Let me get on with it with others,'"* Bettel said.

Incidentally, the Rome summit and subsequently the Rome declaration that it produced (and was signed by all except the UK) marked the 60th anniversary of the European Union.

118

The German thrive for a more robust, better equipped social and economic Eurozone was interpreted by the new member states as an attempt to isolate them behind an iron curtain again.

The Romanians, although highly susceptible, said *"ok"* reluctantly and warned against the creation of *"exclusive clubs"*.

Hungary's Viktor Orbán seized the opportunity of attacking Brussels again. Posters reading *"Stop Brussels"* were spread all over the country and citizens were conveyed to a survey in which their opinion on the EU was asked.

In April, the survey was being posted to households and it contained six questions on *"what Hungary should do"* about EU policies on immigration and economic issues.

The survey came with a letter from Prime Minister Orbán in which he called on the Hungarians to stand up for national independence and fill out the questionnaire *"to support the government's efforts to combat mistaken proposals on the part of Brussels."*

Hungary could've had the option of considering joining the euro sooner, since it will have to do it someday anyway. So, instead of complaining, Viktor Orbán could try get closer to the Eurozone playground.

Daniel Bartha, Director for Centre for Euro-Atlantic Integration and Democracy detailed in July the ups and downs of such idea. Besides the potential risks of the economic impact and the possible tension with Warsaw and Prague, there are benefits too, he thinks.

"First of all, those European decision-makers and opinion formers criticizing the Hungarian Prime Minister based on his anti-European stance, disintegrating policies and populism will be in deep trouble. The current option of a two speed Europe would be seriously hacked, and he could provide a strong answer to those saying there is not a single strong leader East of the Alps. His European leadership aspirations would be finally boosted.

He would not be risking much with the public as well. The introduction of the euro would not be necessarily against his populist policies."

Poland, whose current animosity against Brussels needs no further explaining, is not only about PiS and euro scepticism.

Some of Polish analysts did not dismiss the idea, but also warned against it being a closed cooperation.

And in a surprising development, in August, Slovakia and The Czech Republic asked for an observer status in the Eurozone. They may have understood what the two-speed Europe is all about.

The solidarity is there

I know that I am conflicting with my own arguments, but although there is little solidarity in Europe today, some solidarity still exists.

It concerns the aid put in place years ago through policies and mechanism agreed by the EU when things were still good and smooth. They are not going to be phased out any time soon, unlike the aid through the Common Agriculture Policy which can be subject to massive cuts after 2020.

The solidarity I'm describing is given through means like *"the civil protection mechanism"* or *"the cohesion funds"*.

The first was put in place was during the flooding that destroyed the historical centre of Prague in 2002.

The mechanism is called EU civil protection mechanism because it intervenes when human lives are at stake and it is one of the little known and almost uncredited for achievements of the EU.

It allows a cooperation between member states via a unique platform on which the pledges to help are posted and from which the needy country chooses what it needs.

The mechanism has been activated several times since 2002, the last one being during the forest fires in South of France in 2017. Most of the people who were saved from the flames don't know that this is a joint European rescue mission.

In order to work, this aid has to be asked for by the country or countries being hit by natural disasters or indeed any other type of catastrophes.

In 2015 Romania was eligible for activating the mechanism after the deadly fire that ravaged a night club in Bucharest and claimed the lives of 65 young people. The catastrophe, which also eventually led to a change of government accused of corruption, produced a large number of wounded, as well.

The government had the option to dispatch the victims abroad through this mechanism, as their number surpassed the capacity of the Romanian medical system. In the end, it chose to deal with it bilaterally and more than 60 cases were treaty, sometimes successfully, abroad.

In addition to the joint help provided by this system, the EU Commission launched in 2017 a reconstruction option paid for by the so-called *"cohesion funds"*. If a country chooses to get this sort of help, it must also activate the demand and get a so called co-financing rate of 95%.

In short, only five percent of the reconstruction cost after a disaster is supported by the country, the rest of the money comes from the EU.

This money comes in addition to another fund, the *"solidarity fund"* and it has been proposed by the EU

Commission after the series of earthquakes that stroke the centre of Italy just recently.

The cohesion funds are very little known and therefore too little appreciated EU wide, except in Poland and some other Eastern European countries.

They are part of the wider regional policy of the EU, a complicated invention, but probably the best ever. The regional funds used to be the star of all EU policy and still are, as they get the most of the money.

Although they are technical, complicated and sometimes difficult to get, they are to be acclaimed for the economic reconstruction of Spain, Portugal and Ireland some thirty years ago.

They have also transformed Poland and made Warsaw a better place that the one we used to know some twenty years back.

Nowadays, the Cohesion Fund concerns Bulgaria, Croatia, Cyprus, the Czech Republic, Estonia, Greece, Hungary, Latvia, Lithuania, Malta, Poland, Portugal, Romania, Slovakia and Slovenia.

It allocates a total of € 63.4 billion up to 2020 to infrastructure projects and the environment. But it is easily taken away if the countries do not respect the budgetary rules of the Eurozone.

Here is an interesting trick that only became available with the enlargement of the Eurozone. In order to keep the money, you must follow the rules. These rules are clearly stated and, although considered stupid by a number of founders of the euro like France, they do still apply.

They are about the German discipline imposed on the euro concerning the public deficit that may not exceed 3% of the GNP. If it does, the situation must be corrected within a time framework imposed by Brussels.

Solidarity is not all money and kindness. It can be a carefully planned scenario and it is still possible as long as the people don't get wise on it.

Together with the regional funds, the ones helping underdeveloped regions, the cohesion funds are a God sent not only for the beneficiaries, but sometimes for those who pay them as well. They can be used as a ransom, among other things.

They are currently the only effective way in which Brussels, following a German idea, can persuade a country like Poland or Hungary to respect the EU laws or the Eurozone constraints.

Hungary has already had part of its funds froze over an excessive deficit problem. Poland was openly threatened in 2015 with cuts of its structural funds when it refused to cooperate on migration issues.

Germany also thought that EU should link the aid given to these countries to their willingness of respecting the rule of law. The idea has not yet been put into practice, but it may be in the near future.

Solidarity has been probably the most important element of the EU integration law and it got bigger and more structured over the years. Contributions are given in order to receive the same thing back or in order to achieve a common goal.

This is the idea behind the regional funds, the social funds and the direct payments for farmers. The solidarity therefore exists as it is clearly stated in the EU Treaties and put into practice through programs managed in Brussels.

Solidarity reaches people in various ways. But not many of them realise that *"EU money"* it also their money to begin with. Sure, some states take more than they pay (net beneficiaries) and some get less (net contributors). But all states contribute to the EU budget which, in turn, pays for these funds.

People fail to understand that their taxes not only contribute to their state funds, but also for the EU's.

During the presidential campaign in France in 2017, people were more shocked about François Fillon using the public funds for the fake employment of his wife than they were about Marine Le Pen creating *"fake jobs"* in the EU Parliament.

Of course, what she did was embezzling EU's money, not ours, the French thought as most of them did not realise that was their money too.

Also, most of the European public opinion did not realise that the money given to Greece during its crisis came from their pockets as well. Some of the people were crossed about EU saving Greece in principle, but they could've been even more so if they knew how much it really meant in terms of taxes.

Take Belgium, for instance. This small country, whose economy relies mostly on services, had to bail out Greece and the bank Dexia in the same time. €11 billion euros were borrowed from the market for Greece while the bailing out of Dexia amounted to €2.9 billion.

In order to be able to pay for all this, the coalition government led by the socialist Elio Di Rupo had to raise taxes. It is now said that Belgium had a saving of €12 billion on the interest expenses of its public debt. This amount apparently corresponds to the difference between the interest charges actually paid by Belgium and the assessment of what they would have been without the crisis in Greece.

But the taxes were there. Belgians understood the part about Dexia, as it was a bank they knew and many of them had saving accounts there. But they were kept in the dark concerning Greece.

In 2015 when Greece refused to reimburse its debt and faced exclusion from the Eurozone, Belgium together with the other countries of the euro almost lost the money. The Belgians found out then, from a quick statement made by the Prime Minister (who now was the liberal Charles Michel) how much the country stood to lose.

But even if the figure was out of the bag, people didn't really understand that the money came from their pockets.

The Eurozone meetings in Brussels were held overnight and we were all waiting for the result. One morning when I had just fallen asleep after such a night, I was woken by a neighbour who was mending a fence.

It's not my habit to quarrel, but somehow I found myself shouting at him to stop making all that noise. I think I said something about having had to work over night and when he replied *"too bad, you should've slept"*, I really lost it.

I am ashamed to say that I started lecturing him about Greece and about how the discussions held overnight were supposed to have saved his pension form being ruined in all that trouble. He was literally unimpressed.

"You may say all you want", he replied. *"Their words don't mean a thing. You can't convince me that politicians have nothing better to do than worry about my pension"*.

I had to admit, he was right in a way because, although in that specific moment someone had worried about the loss of money, most of the time nobody cares. But the point made by him without even knowing it was a different one: people did not understand a thing from the entire drama.

And if the money paid by the member states to the EU budget is going into all these solidarity funds, it also goes back to the member states when it's unspent.

Romania, for example, is one of the few EU countries which cannot attract money from Brussels as it has never been able to draw sufficient eligible projects. The crime benefits both to the ruling politicians of the country and to the other member states.

Brussels has put in place complex mechanism against fraud, so the EU money are difficult to be used elsewhere than for the designated projects. The Romanian politicians therefore did not see the point of taking it.

The other member states are said to be happy to get back the unspent money so they are not pushing the Romanians very hard on using the funds. These are of course things that we cannot really prove or even properly check, but they make some sense.

The beauty of Europe

When this Union of nations began to take shape, form and then political colours it has never intended to be a homogenous bloc of people.

We sometimes tend to forget that when thinking of the EU and finding that it has so many nations, languages, mentalities, cultures and shapes.

The EU was meant to be and in fact really is a mixture of all this kept together by the same values, aspirations and ambitions. It is therefore thrilling to observe how 28 countries can more or less get along the same path, each being more different than the next. That's what makes the beauty of it.

EU was built on solidarity, or at least on the principle of it, this one concept that, as we saw, it is more or less applied today.

EU was built on trust and nations trusted one another on big and small issues. Trust has helped containing conflicts like the ownership of the Gibraltar and the Northern Ireland conflict. But trust, or to be specific too much trust, has led almost to the implosion of the Eurozone and the nowadays quarrels with the Visegrad countries.

EU was built on values of peace and democracy and they have proved to be more than helpful up to a point when we realised that even the old democracies of the EU had their flaws.

EU has managed to more or less bring together 500 million people, although many of them are not aware of it.

And unlike politicians and eurocrats, the rest of the people don't aim to a better integration or to a harmonisation of all countries to the tune of Brussels. Most of them have never heard of EU legislation, EU directives and EU protocols.

People know that they can now freely travel in a more or less safe Schengen zone, they all have the euro as a reference as opposed to the past when the dollar was the reference, they send their children to schools abroad and they work abroad when they feel like it. And when they don't feel like working, there is always a more or less comfortable safety net for them, depending to the country they live in.

People sometimes move from one foreign (but EU) country to the next and find jobs and homes and schools and they don't even know or don't entirely realise that this is thanks to the EU.

People could now more easily divorce when they are nationals of two different countries and they live in a third one.

People have the freedom of thought, religion and speech they fully use and cannot imagine nowadays their lives without it. They don't know or they forget that this was not possible a hundred years ago often in the same countries they live in now.

Above all, we now live in peace. This is a cliché, I know and there is always a war going on somewhere or there is one about to start. We also were at war against the banks and we are now fighting terror (or at least we are supposed to).

But let's be fair! The world is changing fast and we are changing as well because we have to adapt. The Europe of today has adapted to the world changes although this is not always tangible.

Give it time.

Europe is an old lady. She has her habits, her fears, she's stubborn and mean, but she is also full of grace and so fragile. She'll not be the first to move or to react and she will not lead the battle. But she'll follow the others at her own pace, keeping her nostalgias and holding on to the past.

Europe, this old bag, likes to remember the older times when she was richer and more powerful, those times when she ruled the Earth and the seven seas. She's sometimes realistic and therefore sad because those times have gone. She sometimes hopes that these times could come back.

They won't. The old lady has to go on as it is whether she likes it or not. Don't criticise her too much. Respect her for what she used to be and encourage her to last longer than time itself.

Bibliography

1. http://www.europarl.europa.eu/RegData/etudes/BRIE/2015/551346/EPRS_BRI%282015%29551346_EN.pdf
2. http://www.europeanleadershipnetwork.org/how-brexit-is-likely-to-impact-european-security-and-defence_4931.html
3. http://visegradinsight.eu/how-to-troll-europe/
4. http://www.statepowerindex.com
5. https://www.theguardian.com/commentisfree/2014/jul/12/why-good-europeans-despair-jean-claude-juncker-commission
6. http://library.fes.de/pdf-files/id/ipa/13506.pdf

Index

Table of contents

Alte apariții în
Editura Excel XXI Books

Cristina Vasiloiu - În labirintul Uniunii

Un ghid complet privind Uniunea Europeana şi instituțiile sale, cu detalii utile pentru cei ce vor să înţeleagă mecanismele decizionale ale acestei structuri complexe.

Autoarea, un reputat jurnalist, are o bogată experienţă în domeniu şi o cunoaştere în profunzime a instituţiilor Uniunii Europene. Călătoria propusă de Cristina Vasiloiu prin Labirintul Uniunii vă oferă atât amănunte tehnice, cât şi detalii savuroase din viaţa de zi cu zi a celor care vorbesc 'bruxelleza'.,

ISBN: 978-606-94101-2-7

Vasile Baltac - Mituri şi realitate în lumea digitală

O carte care dezbate subiecte de interes privind lumea digitală: lumea digitală este pentru toţi, analfabetismul digital, cine se teme şi cine nu se teme de Facebook, Facebook şi teoria conspiraţiei, revoluţia tehnologică – pericol sau oportunitate?!, calculatorul gândeşte deja ca un om?, unde au dispărut tuburile electronice, potopul digital, prăpastia digitală, eGuvernarea: modă sau necesitate?, oraşul inteligent, preţul (in)competenţei digitale şi alte subiecte de actualitate. Autorul, profesorul universitar Vasile Baltac este o voce autorizată în lumea digitală. A publicat numeroase cărţi şi articole despre calculatoare, tehnologiile informaţiei şi societatea, istoria electronicii, eGuvernare. Predă cursuri la SNSPA şi are o prezenţă apreciată în blogosferă.

ISBN: 978-606-94101-1-0

9 781979 435857